Key Stage 3
Developing Numeracy
CALCULATIONS

ACTIVITIES FOR TEACHING NUMERACY

year 9

Hilary Koll and Steve Mills

A & C BLACK

Contents

Published 2003 by A & C Black Publishers Limited
37 Soho Square, London W1D 3QZ
www.acblack.com

ISBN 0-7136-6470-3

Copyright text © Hilary Koll and Steve Mills, 2003
Copyright illustrations © Brett Hudson, 2003
Copyright cover illustration © Paul Cemmick, 2003
Editors: Lynne Williamson and Marie Lister

The authors and publishers would like to thank David Chadwick, Corinne McCrum and Jane McNeill for their advice in producing this series of books.

A CIP catalogue record for this book is available from the British Library.

Printed in Great Britain by St Edmundsbury Press Ltd, Bury St Edmunds, Suffolk.

A & C Black uses paper produced with elemental chlorine-free pulp, harvested from managed sustainable forests.

Introduction

Key Stage 3 **Developing Numeracy: Calculations** is a series of photocopiable resources for Years 7, 8 and 9, designed to be used during maths lessons. The books focus on the Calculations strand of the Key Stage 3 National Strategy *Framework for teaching mathematics*.

Each book supports the teaching of mathematics by providing a series of activities that develop essential skills in numeracy. The activities aim to reinforce learning and develop the skills and understanding explored during whole-class teaching. Each task provides practice and consolidation of an objective contained in the framework document. On the whole the activities are designed for pupils to work on independently, either individually or in pairs, although occasionally some pupils may need support.

The activities in **Calculations Year 9** relate to the following topics:

- number operations and the relationships between them;
- mental methods and rapid recall of number facts;
- written methods;
- calculator methods;
- checking results.

How to use this book

Each double-page spread is based around a Year 9 objective. The spread has three main sections labelled A, B and C, and ends with a challenge (**Now try this!**). The work grows increasingly difficult from A through to C, and the 'Now try this!' challenge reinforces and extends pupils' learning. The activities provide the teacher with an opportunity to make informal assessments: for example, checking that pupils are developing mental strategies, have grasped the main teaching points, or whether they have any misunderstandings.

This double-page structure can be used in a variety of ways: for example, following whole-class teaching the pupils can begin to work through both sheets and will experience gradually more complex questions, or the teacher can choose the most appropriate starting points for each group in the class, with some pupils starting at A and others at B or C. This allows differentiation for mixed-ability groups. 'Now try this!' provides a greater challenge for more able pupils. It can involve 'Using and Applying' concepts and skills, and provides an opportunity for classroom discussion. Where appropriate, pupils can be asked to finish tasks for homework.

The instructions are presented clearly to enable pupils to work independently. There are also opportunities for pupils to work in pairs and groups, to encourage discussion and co-operation. A calculator icon indicates whether or not calculators should be used for different parts of the activities. Where there is no icon, the teacher or pupils may choose whether or not to use them. Brief notes are provided at the foot of each page to assist the pupil or classroom assistant, or parent if the sheets are used for homework. Remind the pupils to read these before beginning the activity.

In some cases, the pupils will need to record their workings on a separate piece of paper, and it is suggested that these workings are handed in with the activity sheets. The pupils will also need to record their answers to some of the 'Now try this!' challenges on another piece of paper.

Organisation

Very little equipment is needed, other than the essential rulers, pencils and so on, but for some activity sheets pupils will need algebraic calculators. These activity sheets allow opportunities for pupils to explore keys and interpret the display on the calculator, considering issues such as rounding. It is important in some cases that the calculators used have certain keys, for example a sign change key. During the teaching input, discuss how such keys can be shown in different ways on different calculators, for example $+/-$ or $(-)$.

To help teachers select appropriate learning experiences for pupils, the activities are grouped into sections within the book to match the objectives in the Key Stage 3 National Strategy *Yearly teaching programmes*. However, the activities do not have to be used in the order given. The sheets are intended to support, rather than direct, the teacher's planning.

Some activities can be made easier or more challenging by masking or substituting some of the numbers. You may wish to re-use some pages by copying them onto card and laminating them, or by enlarging them onto A3 paper. They could also be made into OHTs for whole-class use.

Teachers' notes

Further brief notes, containing specific instructions or points to be raised during the first part of the lesson, are provided for particular sheets (see pages 6–7).

Whole-class oral and mental starters

The following activities provide some practical ideas to support the main teaching part of the lesson, and can be carried out before the pupils use the activity sheets.

Mental methods and rapid recall of number facts

Four eights

Ask pupils to use four number 8s and arrange them in conjunction with operation signs to make any of the numbers between 1 and 20: for example, $3 = (8 + 8 + 8) \div 8$, $4 = (8 \times 8) \div (8 + 8)$. Discuss which numbers between 1 and 20 are impossible to make with four 8s, and explain the reasons for this. Other numbers can be explored in the same way (for example, using four number 4s).

Ratio challenge

Split the class into teams. Ask pupils to write multiples of 40 on the board. Call out a ratio where the numbers add to make a factor of 40 (such as 1 : 9, 3 : 5, 1 : 4, 1 : 3, 2 : 3, 3 : 7) and ask a pupil from each team to choose a number from the board to create a ratio question: for example, *Split 160 in the ratio 1 : 4.* The team should then find the two values mentally (32 and 128). If the answer is correct, the team scores a point.

Complements

Call out positive whole numbers and ask pupils to give the complements to 1000: for example, if you call out 720, the pupils should respond with 280, as $720 + 280 = 1000$. Similarly, decimals (with one or two decimal places) can be called out and pupils asked to give complements to 10: for example, 6.8 and 3.2, or 7.54 and 2.46.

Speed limits

Write the number 30, 40, 60 or 70 in a circle on the board. Explain that this is the 'speed limit'. Ask calculation questions and have pupils say whether the answer is greater than the speed limit ('Speeding'), exactly on the speed limit ('OK') or under the speed limit ('Slow'). Questions could include multiplication and division facts, doubles and halves, and addition and subtraction questions. For example, *I'm travelling at a speed which is 6 times faster than 8 miles per hour, ... half as fast as 76 mph, ... 17 miles per hour slower than 61 mph.*

Written methods

Write it

Split the class into two teams and give each team a digit card, for example 4 and 7. Write a question (using any operation) on the board, to be solved using a column method.

Explain that the teams will score a point each time their digit appears in the written method. Invite a pupil to complete the method on the board and award the points. The teams can choose their own digit once a question is written, if preferred.

Calculator methods

Calculator clues

Write a number fact with some of the digits replaced by blanks, for example □3□4 ÷ □36 = 1□. Ask the pupils to use their calculators to find the missing digits to make a correct number fact. Encourage them to look for clues: for example, $24 \div 6$ gives the unit digit 4 so this must be the units digit of the answer.

Teachers' notes
Number operations and the relationships between them

Pages 8 & 9

The first activity in part C is designed to demonstrate that dividing by zero has no meaning. As you divide a positive number by positive numbers tending towards zero, the answer gets incredibly large. As you divide it by negative numbers tending towards zero, the answer gets incredibly small. Thus what lies between, i.e. dividing by zero, must be somewhere between incredibly large and incredibly small, which has no real meaning. This is a difficult concept, and pupils often confuse it with dividing zero by a number (for example $0 \div 2$, which can be done).

Pages 10 & 11

Revise the greater than/less than signs during the first part of the lesson and introduce a letter on one side of the sign to stand for a range of numbers, for example $x > 4$, where x is any number greater than 4.

Pages 12 & 13

The pupils will need to be familiar with grouping like terms for the questions in part C, for example $3a + 2a = 5a$.

Pages 14 & 15

Pupils should be introduced to the reciprocal key $\boxed{x^{-1}}$ on the calculator and encouraged to realise that this is the same as performing $1 \div x$. Demonstrate this by asking them to key in 4 followed by $\boxed{x^{-1}}$ and then to key in $1 \div 4$. Both ways give the same answer.

Pages 16 & 17

It is important the pupils understand that an inverse operation can undo a previous operation, for example a square root can be undone by squaring. Revise the inverses of the four rules, showing alternative methods: for example, when multiplying a number by $\frac{1}{2}$, the inverse could be multiplying by 2 or dividing by $\frac{1}{2}$. Demonstrate that the inverse of multiplying by $\frac{5}{6}$ can be multiplying by $\frac{6}{5}$. Remind pupils that when a number of operations take place, the order of the inverse operations should be reversed.

Pages 18 & 19

Some teachers prefer to introduce pupils to the term BIDMAS rather than BODMAS, where the 'I' stands for 'indices'. Discuss this with the class and explain that either word can remind them of the order of precedence of operations.

The pupils will require an algebraic calculator with sign change, brackets, square, cube and root keys. In part B, remind the pupils to put brackets around both what is on the top and what is on the bottom of the division line, if they are doing the calculation in one go. Alternatively, they should write the solution to each part first and then do a final calculation.

Mental methods and rapid recall of number facts

Pages 20 & 21

In the plenary session, ask pupils to describe the strategies they used to answer the questions in part A. Invite them to show any jottings they made on the board. Compare different approaches to the same question, asking them to say which approach is most efficient or effective. Pupils tackling part C need to be confident with simple ideas of algebra and substitution. Remind them that when substituting a number for d into the expression $6d$, this means $6 \times d$ and not that 6 is the tens digit and d stands for the units digit, i.e. if d is 3, $6d$ equals 18, not 63.

Pages 22 & 23

Revise the following strategy for finding the prime factors of a number. Divide the number by a prime factor (a number that is prime and divides exactly into the first number). Write down this prime factor and the result of the division. Now divide this result by another prime factor. Continue in this way until a prime number result is reached, for example:

84 divide by 2 = 42

42 divide by 2 = 21

21 divide by 3 = 7

7 is a prime number. So, the prime factors of 84 are 2, 2, 3 and 7. Show that this can be written as $84 = 2^2 \times 3 \times 7$

Pages 28 & 29

Remind the pupils that pi (π) is the symbol for the relationship between the circumference of a circle and its diameter, and that it also shows the relationship between the area of a circle and its radius squared. Watch out for pupils who confuse squaring with doubling. It is common for pupils to think that 9^2 is 18, and so on.

In the 'Now try this!' challenge, ask pupils to discuss which tin gives the most volume for the least amount of aluminium.

Pages 30 & 31

Encourage pupils to appreciate that fractions, decimals and percentages are different ways of expressing the same idea. Explain that this is like three languages: in the 'fraction language' we might say $\frac{3}{4}$, in the 'decimal language' we would say 0.75 and in the 'percentage language' we'd say 75%.

Pages 32 & 33

For part C, ensure pupils understand that the same rule is used for each row in a table. Encourage pupils to find a possible rule by looking at only the first row, and then to test their rule by checking with the numbers in the second and third rows. When pupils have made their own puzzles, they can be checked and written onto cards to be passed around the class, or kept for future activities.

Pages 36 & 37

When pupils are tackling part C, encourage them to make their own decisions about whether to round to the nearest 10, 100, 1000, and so on.

Written methods

For all written calculations, emphasise the importance of making an approximation before the calculation and checking the result afterwards.

Pages 38 & 39

If appropriate, the pupils can be introduced to the idea of rounding to one significant figure when approximating.

Pages 40 & 41

In part B, ensure that the pupils record their written methods of multiplication on paper and attach it to the sheet to enable you to check their methods. Alternatively, they could use the back of the sheet for their workings.

Pages 44 & 45

When completing the calculations in part A, encourage the pupils to examine them carefully. Pupils may be surprised to find that the further Maurice Greene runs, the faster his average speed. To explain this, point out that he spends a greater proportion of his shorter journey building up to his maximum speed, whereas for a greater distance he spends a smaller proportion of the journey at this slower speed and a greater proportion at his maximum speed.

Calculator methods

For all calculations performed on a calculator, emphasise the importance of making an approximation before the calculation and checking the result afterwards.

Pages 48 & 49

In part C, remind the pupils to put brackets around both what is on the top and what is on the bottom of the division line, if they are doing the calculation in one go. Alternatively, they should write the solution to each part first and then do a final calculation.

Pages 50 & 51

Pupils will require calculators with a fraction/decimal key, usually marked $a^{b/_c}$. Demonstrate the use of this key by entering times in hours and minutes. Remind the pupils that minutes should be treated as parts out of 60. Thus, 6 hours and 25 minutes is entered as 6 $a^{b/_c}$ 25 $a^{b/_c}$ 60. After multiplying by 4 and pressing the $=$ key, pressing the $a^{b/_c}$ key again will change the fraction to the decimal 25.6666, the time in hours. Give plenty of experience of this during the first part of the lesson.

Pages 52 & 53

Remind the pupils that pi (π) is the symbol for the relationship between the circumference of a circle and its diameter, and that it also shows the relationship between the area of a circle and its radius squared. For pupils tackling part C, ensure that they work slowly, making a rough approximation of the size of the answer before beginning each part. Remind them of BODMAS to ensure that the calculations are performed in the correct order. Some pupils will benefit from working next to a partner and discussing the order as they both key in the calculations.

Pages 54 & 55

These activities address aspects of the Using and Applying Mathematics strand of the Framework. It is important that pupils communicate their findings. After pupils have completed the 'Now try this!' challenge, ask them to write a report explaining how 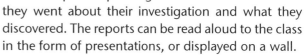 they went about their investigation and what they discovered. The reports can be read aloud to the class in the form of presentations, or displayed on a wall.

Checking results

Pages 56 & 57

Teach each of the different checking strategies separately: for example, using odd and even rules, looking at the last digit, doing an approximation. When several strategies have been taught, provide questions and possible answers on the board. Ask pupils to suggest which checking strategies they might choose and to explain their reasons.

Pages 58 & 59

The pupils can be encouraged to use any appropriate method for answering the questions in part C. During the plenary session, discuss the different methods used.

Larger or smaller?

A

1. Answer these questions. Round your answers to two decimal places.

(a) 47 × £0.13 = _____

(b) 271 × £0.07 = _____

(c) 378 × £0.83 = _____

(d) 32 m ÷ 0.27 m = _____

(e) 38 m ÷ 0.13 m = _____

(f) 128 m ÷ 0.67 m = _____

2. Look at your answers above. Complete these sentences using the word **larger** or **smaller**.

(a) If I multiply a positive number by a number between 0 and 1 the result will be _____.

(b) If I divide a positive number by a number between 0 and 1 the result will be _____.

3.  **Without** calculating, circle the answer you think is correct for each question. Use what you have written above to help you.

(a) 3927 × 0.07   27489   274.89   5610.89

(b) 6836 × 0.84   5742.24   8138.24   9452.24

(c) 29 × 0.089   325.81   2.581   788.1

(d) 981 ÷ 0.06   557.5   58.86   16 350

(e) 1589 ÷ 0.56   889.84   2837.5   6.95

(f) 297 ÷ 0.048   6187.5   61.75   6.175

4. Check your answers to question 3.

B

The number missing from this question is a number between zero and one, with one decimal place.

48 × ☐ =

(a) Will the answer to the question be greater than or less than 48? _____

(b) Write all the possible solutions, to check whether your answer to (a) is correct.

48 × ☐ 0.1 = _4.8_   48 × ☐ = _____   48 × ☐ = _____

48 × ☐ = _____   48 × ☐ = _____   48 × ☐ = _____

48 × ☐ = _____   48 × ☐ = _____   48 × ☐ = _____

You may use a calculator for part B, but look carefully at each answer to see whether you can predict the approximate size of the next answer. This will help you to be sure that your answers are correct.

Developing Numeracy
Calculations
Year 9
© A & C BLACK

Larger or smaller?

1. In this pattern, the number 27 is divided by numbers getting increasingly closer to zero, then by numbers the other side of zero getting increasingly further away.

Continue the pattern.

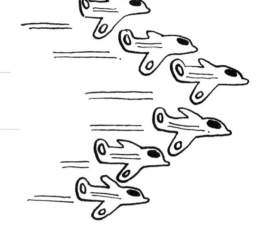

27 ÷ 0.1 = _270_

27 ÷ 0.01 = _2700_

27 ÷ 0.001 = _____

27 ÷ 0.0001 = _____

27 ÷ 0.00001 = _____

27 ÷ 0.000001 = _____

27 ÷ 0.0000001 = _____

27 ÷ 0.00000001 = _____

27 ÷ 0

27 ÷ ⁻0.00000001 = _____

27 ÷ ⁻0.0000001 = _____

27 ÷ ⁻0.000001 = _____

27 ÷ ⁻0.00001 = _____

27 ÷ ⁻0.0001 = _____

27 ÷ ⁻0.001 = _____

27 ÷ ⁻0.01 = _____

27 ÷ ⁻0.1 = _____

2. Look at your answers above. Complete these sentences using the words **infinitely large** or **infinitely small**.

(a) As a positive number is divided by positive decimals approaching zero, the result becomes

_____

(b) As a positive number is divided by negative decimals approaching zero, the result becomes

_____

3. Talk to a partner about why dividing by zero has no meaning.

● Write at least 10 different number statements with the answer 0. Remember, you can divide zero by a number, but you cannot divide a number by zero!

Examples: *0 ÷ 5 = 0   16 × 0 = 0   0 × 16 = 0*

If you try dividing a number by zero on your calculator, it will probably tell you that you have made an error! This is because dividing a number by zero is like asking 'how many lots of zero are there in this number?'

Greater or less than

A For each ⬚inequality⬚, write five numbers (integers or decimals) that *x* could be. Then write five numbers that *x* could **not** be.

		x could be			*x* could not be	
(a)	*x* < 4	2.6 ⁻16			4.1 99	
(b)	*x* > 1					
(c)	*x* > 0					
(d)	0 < *x* < 5					
(e)	*x* > ⁻1					
(f)	*x* < ⁻6					
(g)	0 < *x* < 1					
(h)	⁻2 < *x* < ⁻1					

B Give possible numbers for *a* and *b* in the same way.

		a could be		*a* could not be
(a)	0 < *a* < 1			

		b could be		*b* could not be
(b)	0 < *b* < 1			

Now write statements about the size of answers to these questions. Use a calculator to test your answers if necessary.

> Substitute your possible values for *a* and *b* into the expressions to help you. **!**

(c) *a* + *b*   *The answer must be between 0 and 2.*

(d) *a* × *b* _____

(e) a^2 _____

(f) *a* − *b* _____

(g) 3*b* _____

(h) $(a \times b)^2$ _____

(i) $(a + b)^2$ _____

 An **inequality** is an expression which shows that two quantities are not equal. Remember that integers are whole numbers and they can be positive or negative. In part B, substitute numbers into the expressions, then find the answer and note its size. Try this for the largest and smallest possible values of *a* and *b*, to check your answer range.

Greater or less than

1. Complete these **inequalities**. Fill in the < or > sign and a number.

(a) If $a > 7$ then $2a$ ___> 14___

(b) If $b < 5$ then $2b$ _____

(c) If $c > 3$ then $5c$ _____

(d) If $d > {}^-5$ then $3d$ _____

(e) If $0 < e < 2$ then $0 < e^2$ _____

(f) If $0 < f < 1$ then $0 < f^2$ _____

(g) If $0 < x < 1$ and $0 < y < 1$ then $0 < xy$ _____

(h) If $p > 1$ and $q > 1$ then pq _____

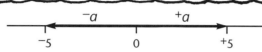

The letter a is a positive whole number and $a < 5$. (So a could be 1, 2, 3 or 4.)

A common error is to say that if $a < 5$ then ${}^-a < {}^-5$. This is incorrect.

If a is 1, 2, 3 or 4, then ${}^-a$ must be ${}^-1$, ${}^-2$, ${}^-3$ or ${}^-4$.

If the lowest ${}^-a$ can be is ${}^-4$, then ${}^-a$ must be **larger** than ${}^-5$, not smaller.

The correct statement is: if $a < 5$ then ${}^-a > {}^-5$.

Notice that the < sign changes.

2. Talk to a partner about the explanation above
and make sure you understand it.

3. Use the explanation to help you complete these inequalities.

(a) If $a > 6$ then ${}^-a$ ___< ${}^-6$___

(b) If $b < 4$ then ${}^-b$ _____

(c) If $c < 9$ then ${}^-c$ _____

(d) If $d > 1$ then ${}^-d$ _____

NOW TRY THIS!

● Tick the true inequalities.

(a) If $s > 1$ and $t > 1$, which of these are true? Tick them.

${}^-s > {}^-1$ ☐	${}^-t > {}^-1$ ☐	$st < s$ ☐	$st < t$ ☐	${}^-s < {}^-1$ ☐
$st > s$ ☐	$st > t$ ☐	$st > 1$ ☐	$st < 1$ ☐	${}^-t < {}^-1$ ☐

(b) If $s > 1$ and $t > 1$ and $s > t$, which of these are true?

$\frac{s}{t} > 1$ ☐ $\frac{s}{t} < 1$ ☐ $\frac{t}{s} > 1$ ☐ $\frac{t}{s} < 1$ ☐

To help you find answers to these questions, try substituting numbers into
the expressions. Find the answer and note its size. Try this for the largest
and smallest possible values, to check your answer range.

Follow the laws

A

1. Use the ⟨commutative law⟩ and the ⟨associative law⟩ to help you answer these questions. Do the calculations in your head.

(a) $4.5 \times 0.8 \times 2 =$ _____

(b) $25 \times 33 \times 8 =$ _____

(c) $7.5 \times 4 \times 8 =$ _____

(d) $12 \times 7.5 \times 4 =$ _____

(e) $2.8 \times 0.2 \times 5 =$ _____

(f) $24 \times 4 \times 0.5 =$ _____

(g) $11 \times 7.5 \times 8 =$ _____

(h) $4 \times 4.5 \times 4.5 =$ _____

(i) $3.5 \times 8 \times 2 =$ _____

2. Find the volume of each cuboid. Calculate in your head. ⟩ Volume of cuboid = $l \times h \times w$

(a)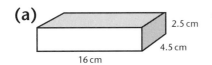
2.5 cm
4.5 cm
16 cm

(b)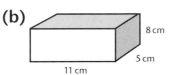
8 cm
5 cm
11 cm

(c)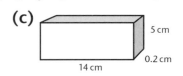
5 cm
0.2 cm
14 cm

Volume = _____

Volume = _____

Volume = _____

(d)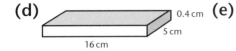
0.4 cm
5 cm
16 cm

(e)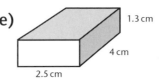
1.3 cm
4 cm
2.5 cm

(f)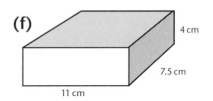
4 cm
7.5 cm
11 cm

Volume = _____

Volume = _____

Volume = _____

B

When you multiply two-digit numbers informally, you can **partition** them and multiply each part separately. Then find the total.

Example: $27 \times 14 = (20 + 7) \times (10 + 4)$
$= (20 \times 10) + (20 \times 4) + (7 \times 10) + (7 \times 4)$
$= 200 + 80 + 70 + 28 = 378$

Try these multiplications using the method above.

(a) $44 \times 13 = (40 + 4) \times (10 + 3) = (40 \times 10) + (40 \times 3) + (4 \times 10) + (4 \times 3)$

$= \quad + \quad + \quad + \quad =$

(b) $26 \times 17 =$ _____

_____

(c) $32 \times 14 =$ _____

_____

(d) $26 \times 15 =$ _____

_____

(e) $55 \times 18 =$ _____

_____

The **commutative law** of multiplication means that you can multiply numbers in any order and the answer will be the same. The **associative law** says that when you multiply more than two numbers together, you can group them in any way and the answer will be the same. **Partitioning** is splitting a number into parts to make the calculation easier.

Developing Numeracy
Calculations
Year 9
© A & C BLACK

Follow the laws

C The **distributive law** states that when you multiply two sets of brackets, such as $(a + 2)(a + 3)$, you can multiply each part of one bracket by each part of the other, then add the results.

Here are two different ways of doing this.

Draw a multiplication grid like this:

$\times$	a	$+\,3$
a	a^2	$3a$
$+\,2$	$2a$	6

$= a^2 + 5a + 6$

Draw two eyebrows, a nose and a mouth and multiply the parts joined by a line.

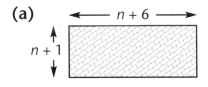

$(a + 2)\,(a + 3) = a^2 + 6 + 3a + 2a$
$\qquad\qquad\qquad = a^2 + 5a + 6$

1. Use one or both of the methods above to multiply these brackets. Show your workings.

(a) $(a + 4)\,(a + 6)$

(b) $(b + 5)\,(b + 4)$

(c) $(c + 3)\,(9 + c)$

(d) $(11 + d)\,(d + 7)$

(e) $(x + y)\,(x + y)$

(f) $(y + 1)\,(y - 1)$

2. Find the area of each rectangle in terms of n.

(a)

$\longleftarrow\ n + 6\ \longrightarrow$
$n + 1$

Area = _____

(b)

$\longleftarrow\ n + 7\ \longrightarrow$
$n + 2$

Area = _____

(c)

$\longleftarrow\ n + 10\ \longrightarrow$
$n - 1$

Area = _____

(d)

$\longleftarrow\ n + 5\ \longrightarrow$
$n - 5$

Area = _____

NOW TRY THIS!

● The length of one side of the square is given. Find the area of each square in terms of n.

(a) $n + 2$ **(b)** $n + 5$ **(c)** $n - 3$ **(d)** $n - 11$

_____   _____   _____   _____

The **distributive law** of multiplication means that you can split one of the things you are multiplying into parts (for example, split $a + 2$ into a and 2) and multiply each part separately. Then add the results together to get the answer.

Find the reciprocal

A

Under each of these flaps is a number. The product of the two numbers is 1.

$$\boxed{} \times \boxed{} = 1$$

1. Write twelve different pairs of numbers that could be hidden beneath the flaps.

(a) $\boxed{1} \times \boxed{1} = 1$ (b) $\boxed{} \times \boxed{} = 1$

(c) $\boxed{} \times \boxed{} = 1$ (d) $\boxed{} \times \boxed{} = 1$

(e) $\boxed{} \times \boxed{} = 1$ (f) $\boxed{} \times \boxed{} = 1$

(g) $\boxed{} \times \boxed{} = 1$ (h) $\boxed{} \times \boxed{} = 1$

(i) $\boxed{} \times \boxed{} = 1$ (j) $\boxed{} \times \boxed{} = 1$

(k) $\boxed{} \times \boxed{} = 1$ (l) $\boxed{} \times \boxed{} = 1$

! The numbers could be fractions, decimals or negative numbers.

When two numbers have a product of 1, one number is called the $\boxed{\text{reciprocal}}$ of the other.
The reciprocal of any number is 1 divided by the number.

B

1. Tick the expressions that give the answer 1.

(a) $\frac{1}{9} \times 9$ ✔

(b) $\frac{1}{14} \times 14$

(c) $4 \times \frac{3}{4}$

(d) 0.125×8

(e) $10 \times \frac{1}{5}$

(f) $\frac{1}{a} \times a$

(g) $b \times \frac{1}{b}$

(h) $\frac{c}{1} \times c$

2. Find the reciprocal of the numbers below. Ask yourself:

What must I multiply this number by to get 1?

Write your answers as whole numbers or fractions.

(a) $\frac{1}{2}$ 2   (b) $\frac{1}{4}$ _____   (c) 12 _____   (d) 10 _____

(e) 27 _____   (f) $\frac{1}{15}$ _____   (g) $\frac{1}{7}$ _____   (h) 56 _____

(i) 121 _____   (j) 0.01 _____   (k) $\frac{1}{16}$ _____   (l) $\frac{1}{3}$ _____

3. 🖩 Now check your answers by multiplying the two numbers.

When you are using a calculator, you can find the **reciprocal** of a number by dividing 1 by the number. You can also use the reciprocal key if your calculator has one: enter any number, press $\boxed{x^{\text{-}}}$ and you will get its reciprocal. You can then change this to a fraction, if you wish, by pressing $\boxed{a^{b/c}}$.

Developing Numeracy
Calculations
Year 9
© A & C BLACK

Find the reciprocal

C

1. Find the **reciprocal** of each number by dividing 1 by the given number. Write your answer as a whole number or as a decimal rounded to three decimal places.

(a) 4 _____   **(b)** 10 _____   **(c)** 8 _____   **(d)** 5 _____

(e) 3 _____   **(f)** 0.02 _____   **(g)** 25 _____   **(h)** 18 _____

(i) 0.01 _____   **(j)** 0.001 _____   **(k)** 7 _____   **(l)** 0.3 _____

2. Now check your answers by multiplying the two numbers.

> Remember: some of your reciprocals are approximate ones.

!

3. Find the reciprocals of these numbers.

(a) 0.0625 _____   **(b)** 16 _____

4. Write what this tells you about reciprocals. _____

_____

5. These people are thinking of whole numbers between 1 and 50. Use the $\boxed{x^{-1}}$ key to work out which numbers they are thinking of.

> Remember: for any number, x, its reciprocal will be $\frac{1}{x}$, which is the same as x^{-1}.

!

(a)
The reciprocal of my number is 0.03125.

(b)
The reciprocal of my number to two decimal places is 0.09.

(c)
The reciprocal of my number to three decimal places is 0.023.

(d)
The reciprocal of my number to three decimal places is 0.036.

(e)
The reciprocal of my number to three decimal places is 0.028.

(f)
The reciprocal of my number to three decimal places is 0.048.

NOW TRY THIS!

• Fill in the missing digits to make this statement correct.

| 4 | is the reciprocal of | 0 | . | 0 | 1 | | 2 | 5 |

 When you are using a calculator, you can find the **reciprocal** of a number by dividing 1 by the number. You can also use the reciprocal key if your calculator has one: enter any number, press $\boxed{x^{-1}}$ and you will get its reciprocal. You can then change this to a fraction, if you wish, by pressing $\boxed{a^{b}/_{c}}$.

Get back!

A

1. Below are some calculations Leah has done on her calculator. How can she undo the operation without pressing cancel and starting again?

(a) $814 \div 0.7 = $ | x | . | 7 | $=$ |

(b) $814 \times 89 = $ ☐☐☐☐☐

(c) $814 \times \frac{1}{4} = $ ☐☐☐

(d) $814^2 = $ ☐☐

(e) $\sqrt{814} = $ ☐☐

(f) $814^3 = $ ☐☐

(g) $\sqrt[3]{814} = $ ☐☐

(h) $814 \div \frac{1}{9} = $ ☐☐☐

(i) $814 \times \frac{7}{8} = $ ☐☐☐☐☐☐

(j) $814 \div \frac{5}{9} = $ ☐☐☐☐☐☐

> **!** You might not need to use all the boxes, or you might need to draw more.

2. Write the ⌊ inverse ⌋ of each number chain.

(a)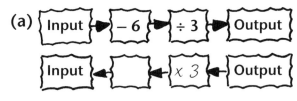

Input → −6 → ÷3 → Output

Input ← ☐ ← ×3 ← Output

(b)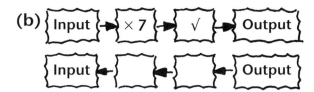

Input → ×7 → √ → Output

Input ← ☐ ← ☐ ← Output

(c)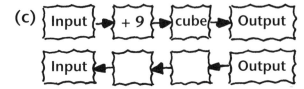

Input → +9 → cube → Output

Input ← ☐ ← ☐ ← Output

(d)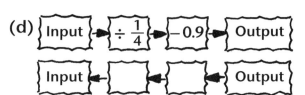

Input → ÷$\frac{1}{4}$ → −0.9 → Output

Input ← ☐ ← ☐ ← Output

B

Use inverse operations to find the value of a in each equation. Work back through the question from the answer.

(a) $(a - 5) \times 2 = 16$

$16 \to$ ÷2 $\to$ +5 $\to 13$

(b) $(a + 1) \div 5 = 6$

$6 \to$ ☐ $\to$ ☐ $\to$

(c) $(a \times 8) - 4 = 12$

$\to$ ☐ $\to$ ☐ $\to$

(d) $a^2 + 5 = 30$

$\to$ ☐ $\to$ ☐ $\to$

(e) $(a \div 2) \times \frac{1}{4} = 3$

$\to$ ☐ $\to$ ☐ $\to$

(f) $\sqrt{a} + 9 = 13$

$\to$ ☐ $\to$ ☐ $\to$

(g) $(a \div 6.4) - 2 = 8$

$\to$ ☐ $\to$ ☐ $\to$

(h) $a^2 + 0.84 = 1$

$\to$ ☐ $\to$ ☐ $\to$

(i) $(a^3 + 5) \div 4 = 8$

$\to$ ☐ $\to$ ☐ $\to$ ☐ $\to$

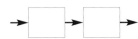 The **inverse** of an operation is the operation that has the opposite effect (for example, addition is the inverse of subtraction; squaring is the inverse of finding the square root). Check each of your answers to part B by substituting your value for a into the equation. Work through the question to check that you reach the given answer.

Developing Numeracy
Calculations
Year 9
© A & C BLACK

Get back!

C

1. **(a)** Write the **inverse** of this number chain.

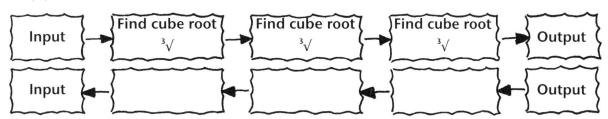

| Input | → | Find cube root $\sqrt[3]{}$ | → | Find cube root $\sqrt[3]{}$ | → | Find cube root $\sqrt[3]{}$ | → | Output |

| Input | ← | | ← | | ← | | ← | Output |

(b) Input the number 8 into the first chain and write down the output number. Key in the output number and work back through the second chain.

Do you return to your input number?　　Yes ☐　　No ☐

(c) Input these numbers in the same way and check by working back through the second chain.

9　　　　55　　　　988　　　　599　　　　844

Do you always return to your input number?　　Yes ☐　　No ☐

(d) Explain why you think this is. _____

_____

_____

(e) Circle the single-digit numbers that do **not** return exactly to their input number.

1　　2　　3　　4　　5　　6　　7　　8　　9

2. Tick to show which of these statements are true.

(a)  If $a^2 = b$, then $\sqrt{b} = a$ ☐

(b) If $a \times b = c$, then $a \div c = b$ ☐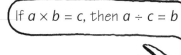

(c) If $a^3 = c$, then $\sqrt[3]{c} = a$ ☐

(d) If $\dfrac{a}{b} = c$, then $c \times b = a$ ☐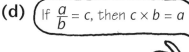

(e) Discuss your reasoning with a partner.

NOW TRY THIS!

• Rewrite these equations in terms of a. Work backwards from the letter c and use inverse operations. Simplify where possible.

(a) $(a - b) \div 4 = c$　　　　**(b)** $(a + 5) \times b = c$　　　　**(c)** $(a + b)^2 = c$

$a = 4c + b$

The **inverse** of an operation is the operation that has the opposite effect (for example, squaring is the inverse of finding the square root). Talk to a partner about your explanation for question 1(d). To help you with question 2, choose numbers to stand for the letters and test both equations. Remember that you can also choose negative numbers.

Order, order...

A

The word BODMAS can help you to remember the order of operations.

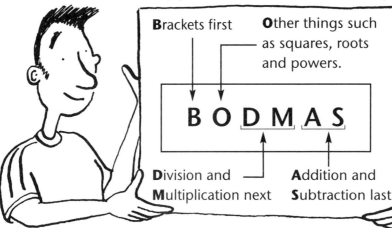

Brackets first   **O**ther things such
as squares, roots
and powers.

B O D M A S

Division and   **A**ddition and
Multiplication next   **S**ubtraction last

> Use cancelling or work
> out the answers mentally. **!**

1. Answer the questions using the order of BODMAS.

(a) $\dfrac{(5 \times 3)^2}{5 \times 3} = \dfrac{15^2}{15} = \dfrac{15 \times 15}{15} = 15$

(b) $\dfrac{5 \times 3^2}{5 \times 3} =$

(c) $\dfrac{(8 + 1)^2}{3^2} =$

(d) $\dfrac{8 + 1^2}{3^2} =$

(e) $\dfrac{2 \times 5^2}{(4 + 1)^2} =$

(f) $\dfrac{(2 \times 5)^2}{(4 + 1)^2} =$

(g) $\dfrac{2 \times 5^2}{4 + 1^2} =$

(h) $\dfrac{(2 \times 5)^2}{4 + 1^2} =$

(i) $\dfrac{\sqrt{(9 + 7)}}{\sqrt{(1 + 3)}} =$

(j) $\dfrac{\sqrt{9} + 7}{\sqrt{(1 + 3)}} =$

2. Answer these questions, calculating in your head. Underline the part you do first.

(a) $48 \div (7 + 5) - 8 + 2 \times (12 \div 6)^3$ _____

(b) $6 + 2 \times (13 - 7)^2 - 5 \times \sqrt{100}$ _____

(c) $(4 + 3)^2 - 4^3 \div 2 + (5 - 4)^3$ _____

(d) $18 \div (10 - 7)^2 + 5 \times \sqrt[3]{(4 \times 2)}$ _____

B

Answer these questions. Give your answers to
two decimal places.

> Remember: when two sets of brackets
> are together, you have to multiply them. **!**

(a) $\dfrac{(13 - 6)^2 (5 + 2)^2}{(5 - 2)^3} = \quad 88.93$

(b) $\dfrac{(15 + 2)^2 (8 - 5)^2}{(8 + 2)^3} =$

(c) $\dfrac{(5 + 3)^2 (7 - 5)^3}{(6 - 3)^3} =$

(d) $\dfrac{(15 - 9)^2 (8 - 5)^3}{\sqrt{(28 + 32)}} =$

(e) $\dfrac{(16 - 9)^3 \times \sqrt{64}}{(17 - 9)^2} =$

(f) $\dfrac{(12 - 9)^3 (1 + 2)^3}{\sqrt{(27 + 56)}} =$

(g) $\dfrac{(14 - 7)^2 (8 - 2)^2}{2(4 + 1)^3} =$

(h) $\dfrac{(4 - 1)^2 (9 - 5)^2}{3(8 - 5)^3} =$

Don't worry if a calculation has only some of the BODMAS operations. Just
continue to follow the order of BODMAS, leaving out any operations that
are missing. Remember to put anything above or below a long division line
in brackets.

Developing Numeracy
Calculations
Year 9
© A & C BLACK

Order, order...

1. Is this statement true? Check using your calculator if you need to.

$(^-3)^2$ gives the same answer as $^-3^2$.

True ☐   False ☐

Explain your answer. _____

_____

2. In each pair of equations, one answer is correct and one is incorrect. Find the incorrect answer and correct it.

If a is 3 then:

(a) $(^-a)^2 = \cancel{^-9}$ 9 $^-a^2 = ^-9$ ✔

(b) $(2a)^2 - 7 = 29$ $2a^2 - 7 = 29$

(c) $^-a^2 + 4 = 13$ $(^-a)^2 + 4 = 13$

(d) $4(a^2 - 1) = 32$ $4a^2 - 1 = 32$

(e) $^-2a^2 + 1 = ^-17$ $(^-2a)^2 + 1 = ^-17$

(f) $3(a^2 + 1) = 30$ $3a^2 + 1 = 30$

(g) $^-4a^2 + 4 = 148$ $(^-4a)^2 + 4 = 148$

(h) $^-5a^2 - 2 = ^-47$ $^-5(a^2 - 2) = ^-47$

(i) $(4a)^2 - 5 = 31$ $4a^2 - 5 = 31$

(j) $\sqrt{(16 \times a + 1)} = 7$ $\sqrt{16} \times a + 1 = 7$

(k) $\sqrt{25} \times a - 11 = 8$ $\sqrt{(25 \times a - 11)} = 8$

(l) $\frac{1}{3} a^3 = 9$ $\left(\frac{1}{3} a\right)^3 = 9$

(m) $(7 + ^-2a)^2 = 43$ $7 + (^-2a)^2 = 43$

Order order!

NOW TRY THIS!

● If $a = ^-3$, find the values of:

(a) $5(a^2 + 2) =$ _____   **(b)** $5a^2 + 2 =$ _____   **(c)** $(5a)^2 + 2 =$ _____

Always look carefully at a calculation and think of BODMAS to see which order you should solve it in. Remember that the **O** in BODMAS reminds you to do 'Other' things such as squares, roots and powers before you do multiplication, division, addition and subtraction.

Key puzzles

A

Here are two different methods for finding unknown multiplication facts.

Multiply by an easier number, such as a multiple of 10 or 25, and then adjust the answer after.

Double one number and halve the other – the answer is the same!

Join each multiplication to its correct answer. Explain your mental method.

728

985

768

1224

984

490

588

880

688

810

3666

360

3366

540

3966

(a) 32 × 24

(b) 24 × 41

(c) 49 × 12

(d) 4.5 × 180

(e) 3.5 × 140

(f) 160 × 5.5

(g) 4.8 × 75

(h) 99 × 34

(i) 21 × 28

I know that 32 × 25 is 800, and 32 less than 800 is 768.

_____

_____

_____

_____

_____

_____

_____

_____

_____

_____

_____

B

Use mental methods to answer these questions.

(a) $900 \times 0.8 =$ _720_   (b) $0.36 \div 0.1 =$ _____   (c) $9 \times 0.04 =$ _____

(d) $48 \times 0.01 =$ _____   (e) $80 \times 0.07 =$ _____   (f) $6400 \div 0.1 =$ _____

(g) $28 \div 0.01 =$ _____   (h) $0.6 \times 0.7 =$ _____   (i) $0.7 \times 700 =$ _____

(j) $0.6 \times 0.08 =$ _____   (k) $0.01 \times 27 =$ _____   (l) $9 \times 0.004 =$ _____

In part B, use number facts you know to help you answer the questions:
for example, for 900×0.8, remember that $9 \times 8 = 72$.

**Developing Numeracy
Calculations
Year 9
© A & C BLACK**

20

Key puzzles

1. This key shows the value of each letter *a* to *h*. Substitute the numbers into the expressions and find the value of each expression.

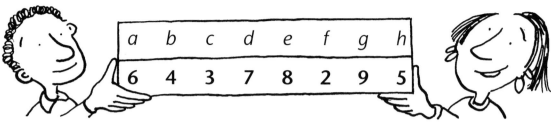

a	b	c	d	e	f	g	h
6	4	3	7	8	2	9	5

(a) $4d + f = \underline{\ 30\ }$

(b) $5g - h = \underline{\hspace{1cm}}$

(c) $a^2 = \underline{\hspace{1cm}}$

(d) $(e + f)^2 = \underline{\hspace{1cm}}$

(e) $d \times e = \underline{\hspace{1cm}}$

(f) $b(c + e) = \underline{\hspace{1cm}}$

(g) $(a + b)(a - b) = \underline{\hspace{1cm}}$

(h) $\sqrt{g} = \underline{\hspace{1cm}}$

(i) $(g - h)^2 = \underline{\hspace{1cm}}$

(j) $6e - 4d = \underline{\hspace{1cm}}$

(k) $h^2 - 2g = \underline{\hspace{1cm}}$

(l) $ab - cd = \underline{\hspace{1cm}}$

(m) $a \times b \times c = \underline{\hspace{1cm}}$

(n) $f \times g \times h = \underline{\hspace{1cm}}$

(o) $d \times e \times f = \underline{\hspace{1cm}}$

(p) $bc \div (f + e) = \underline{\hspace{1cm}}$

(q) $d \times e \div b = \underline{\hspace{1cm}}$

(r) $8e \div b \div f = \underline{\hspace{1cm}}$

2. Solve these puzzles in your head.

> **!** Write down a formula or equation to help you.

(a) The product of two numbers is 48. Their difference is 8. What are the two numbers?

(b) A triangle has an area of 28 cm^2. Its height is 4 cm. How long is its base?

(c) Two consecutive numbers have a product of 182. What are the two numbers?

(d) The mean of a set of eight numbers is 7. Which of the numbers is not listed here? 6, 6, 5, 9, 9, 7, 8

(e) Five angles meet at a point. The angles are all equal. What size are they?

(f) A car travels 28 miles to every gallon of petrol. How many miles will it travel on $12\frac{1}{2}$ gallons?

NOW TRY THIS!

| 3 | 3 | 3 | 3 | | × | ÷ | − | = | (|) |

- Work with a partner.
- Using **all four** 3s, and any of the mathematical signs, make questions with whole number answers between 1 and 10.

Example: $(3 \times 3) + \frac{3}{3} = 10$

Compare your answers to the 'Now try this!' challenge with someone else to see whether you have found different ways of making the same number.

Fast factors

A

Remember: to change a fraction to its simplest form, divide the numerator and denominator by the **highest common factor (HCF)** of the two numbers.

The fractions that meet have to be equal. **!**

1. Complete the domino sequence by writing equivalent fractions in their simplest form.

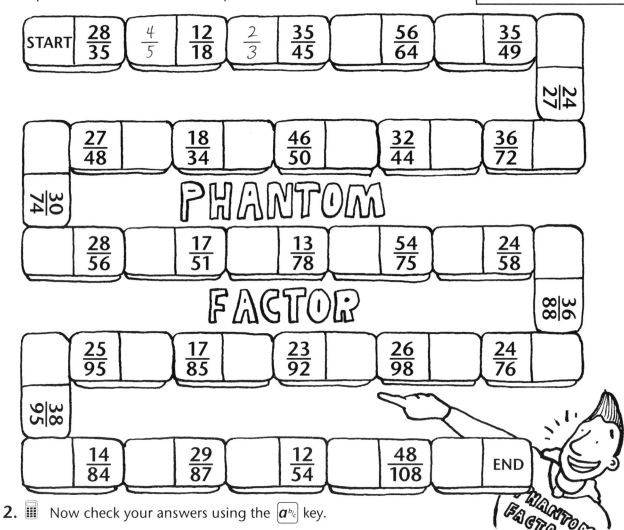

START | $\frac{28}{35}$ | $\frac{4}{5}$ | $\frac{12}{18}$ | $\frac{2}{3}$ | $\frac{35}{45}$ | | $\frac{56}{64}$ | | $\frac{35}{49}$ |

$\frac{24}{27}$

| $\frac{27}{48}$ | | $\frac{18}{34}$ | | $\frac{46}{50}$ | | $\frac{32}{44}$ | | $\frac{36}{72}$ |

$\frac{30}{74}$

PHANTOM

| $\frac{28}{56}$ | | $\frac{17}{51}$ | | $\frac{13}{78}$ | | $\frac{54}{75}$ | | $\frac{24}{58}$ |

FACTOR

$\frac{36}{88}$

| $\frac{25}{95}$ | | $\frac{17}{85}$ | | $\frac{23}{92}$ | | $\frac{26}{98}$ | | $\frac{24}{76}$ |

$\frac{38}{95}$

| $\frac{14}{84}$ | | $\frac{29}{87}$ | | $\frac{12}{54}$ | | $\frac{48}{108}$ | | END |

2. ▦ Now check your answers using the $a^{b}/_{c}$ key.

B

Write the | prime factors | of these numbers and find the highest common factor.

To find the HCF, compare the prime factors of the two numbers. Choose those that they have in common and multiply them together. **!**

(a) (56) = ___$2^3 \times 7$___ and (84) = ___$2^2 \times 3 \times 7$___ HCF is ___$2^2 \times 7 = 28$___

(b) (36) = _____ and (48) = _____ HCF is _____

(c) (14) = _____ and (42) = _____ HCF is _____

(d) (96) = _____ and (84) = _____ HCF is _____

(e) (54) = _____ and (72) = _____ HCF is _____

 To use the $a^{b}/_{c}$ key, press the numerator first, then $a^{b}/_{c}$, then the denominator, followed by $=$. A **factor** is a whole number that divides exactly into another without a remainder. A **prime factor** is a factor that is a prime number. A **prime number** has only two factors, itself and 1. Here are the first ten prime numbers: 2, 3, 5, 7, 11, 13, 17, 19, 23, 29.

Developing Numeracy
Calculations
Year 9
© A & C BLACK

Fast factors

C

1. Play this game with a partner.

Use a calculator to check if necessary. **!**

☆ Take turns to choose two numbers from the grid.

☆ Work out the **highest common factor** of your two numbers and record the answer.
  Example: The HCF of 17 and 34 is 17

☆ Score the same number of points as your highest common factor.

☆ The winner is the first player to reach 100 points.

PHANTOM FACTOR starring in
Highest Common Factor
5.30
7.30
9.30

24	34	25	27	45	36
66	21	17	43	51	28
14	48	54	42	26	55
49	22	39	62	18	63

Workings	My score	My partner's score

2. Which two numbers in the grid have the greatest HCF? _____

NOW TRY THIS!

● Explain in words the difference between the highest common factor and the
  | lowest common multiple | of two numbers.

_____

● Give examples for the numbers 36 and 24.

_____

 A **factor** is a number that divides exactly into another without a remainder.
To find the **highest common factor** of two numbers, first find all the
prime factors of each number (a prime factor is a factor that is a prime
number). Then compare the prime factors of the two numbers. Choose
those that they have in common and multiply them together.

Pyramid power

A Complete the number pyramids. Add each pair of adjacent numbers, **square** the result and write the answer in the brick above.

(a)
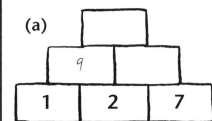

| 9 |
| 1 | 2 | 7 |

(b)

| 3 | 2 | 3 |

(c)

| 3 | 4 | 5 |

B These equations show how much money, in pounds, three contestants will win in a game show.

Sam

$(6 - a)^3$

Baz

$(a + 4)^2$

Kim

$a^3 - 1$

1. Find out how many pounds each contestant will win:

(a) if $a = 3$

Sam $(6 - 3)^3 = 3^3 = £27$ Baz _____   Kim _____

(b) if $a = 1$

Sam _____   Baz _____   Kim _____

(c) if $a = 4$

Sam _____   Baz _____   Kim _____

(d) if $a = 5$

Sam _____   Baz _____   Kim _____

(e) if $a = 2$

Sam _____   Baz _____   Kim _____

(f) if $a = 6$

Sam _____   Baz _____   Kim _____

2. (a) If a could be any number between 0 and 20, which contestant do you think has the best equation? _____

(b) These are possible number ranges for a. Which contestant is each number range best for?

$0 \leq a \leq 2$ $3 \leq a \leq 4$ $5 \leq a \leq 20$

_____   _____   _____

To **square** a number, multiply the number by itself. To square a multiple of ten, first write the number as a number multiplied by ten: for example, write 30 as 3×10. Then square this: $30^2 = 3 \times 3 \times 10 \times 10 = 900$.
To **cube** a number, multiply the number by itself twice (for example, $2^3 = 2 \times 2 \times 2 = 8$).

Developing Numeracy
Calculations
Year 9
© A & C BLACK

Pyramid power

C

1. Complete these number pyramids. Add each pair of adjacent numbers, **square** the result and write the answer in the brick above.

(a)

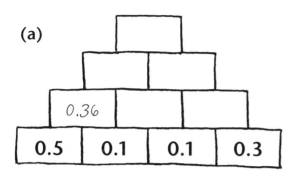

0.36

| 0.5 | 0.1 | 0.1 | 0.3 |

(b)

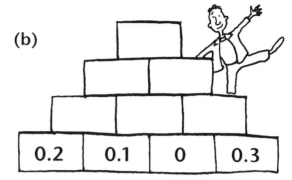

| 0.2 | 0.1 | 0 | 0.3 |

2. Complete these number pyramids. This time, add each pair of adjacent numbers, find the **square root** of the result and write the answer in the brick above.

(a)

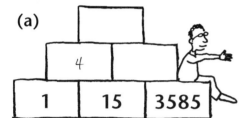

4

| 1 | 15 | 3585 |

(b)

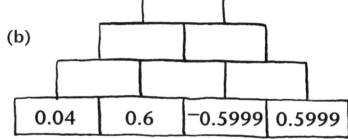

| 0.04 | 0.6 | ‾0.5999 | 0.5999 |

3. Use mental methods to find the value of a in each equation.

(a) $(a + 3)^2 = 36$ $a = 3$

(b) $(a + 2)^2 = 25$ $a =$

(c) $(12 - 9)^2 = a$ $a =$

(d) $(3 \times 4) = \sqrt{a}$ $a =$

(e) $(a + 2)^2 = 81$ $a =$

(f) $(a \times 2)^2 = 64$ $a =$

(g) $(9 - a)^2 = 49$ $a =$

(h) $(6 + a)^2 = 121$ $a =$

(i) $(4 - 2)^3 = a$ $a =$

(j) $(5 - a)^3 = 27$ $a =$

(k) $(3 + a)^3 = 64$ $a =$

(l) $(3 - a) = \sqrt[3]{8}$ $a =$

NOW TRY THIS!

- Solve this puzzle.

  *I'm thinking of a **square number**. If I multiply this number by 8 it becomes a **cube number**. What number am I thinking of?*

- Make up some more puzzles like this for a partner to solve.

To **square** a number, multiply the number by itself. Finding the **square root** is the inverse (opposite) of squaring. A **square number** is a number made by squaring another number: for example, $5 \times 5 = 25$, so 25 is a square number. A **cube number** is a number made by cubing another number: for example, $2 \times 2 \times 2 = 8$, so 8 is a cube number.

Mental measures

A 1. Use mental methods to find the perimeter and area of each rectangle.

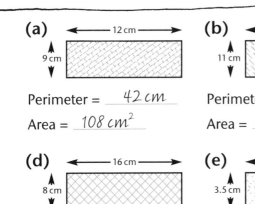

(a) ← 12 cm → / 9 cm

Perimeter = ___42 cm___

Area = ___108 cm²___

(b) ← 13 cm → / 11 cm

Perimeter = _____

Area = _____

(c) ← 15 cm → / 8 cm

Perimeter = _____

Area = _____

(d) ← 16 cm → / 8 cm

Perimeter = _____

Area = _____

(e) ← 14 cm → / 3.5 cm

Perimeter = _____

Area = _____

(f) ← 12 cm → / 5.5 cm

Perimeter = _____

Area = _____

(g) ← 3.2 cm → / 1.1 cm

Perimeter = _____

Area = _____

(h) ← 11 cm → / 2.4 cm

Perimeter = _____

Area = _____

(i) ← 3.5 cm → / 1.5 cm

Perimeter = _____

Area = _____

2. Substitute values into the formula to find the missing measurements. Calculate in your head.

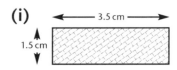

Area of rectangle = $l \times w$

(a) l = 12 cm
w = 4.5 cm   Area = _____

(b) l = 17 cm
w = _____   Area = 51 cm²

(c) l = 16 cm
w = 12.5 cm   Area = _____

(d) l = _____
w = 7.5 cm   Area = 180 cm²

B 1. Substitute values for h and w into the formula to find the area. Calculate in your head.

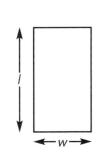

Area of triangle = $\frac{1}{2} \times h \times w$

(a) h = 32 cm
w = 12 cm   Area = _____

(b) h = 24 cm
w = 8 cm   Area = _____

(c) h = 11 cm
w = 2.4 cm   Area = _____

(d) h = 5 cm
w = 3.4 cm   Area = _____

(e) h = 12 cm
w = 7.5 cm   Area = _____

(f) h = 12 cm
w = 16 cm   Area = _____

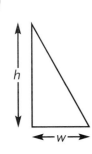

2. What is the width of the triangle if h = 11 cm and the area = 28.6 cm²? _____

Remember to give the correct unit of measurement for each answer.
Perimeter is a measurement of length, so it should be in cm. Area is
a 2-D measurement, so it should be in cm².

Developing Numeracy
Calculations
Year 9
© A & C BLACK

Mental measures

C To find the area of a trapezium, add the parallel sides and halve the answer. Then multiply this by the height.

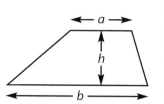

$$\text{Area of trapezium} = \tfrac{1}{2}(a + b) \times h$$

1. Use mental methods to find the area of each trapezium.

(a)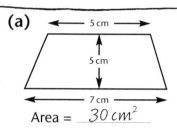
5 cm
5 cm
7 cm
Area = _30 cm²_

(b)
4 cm
8 cm
9 cm
Area = _____

(c)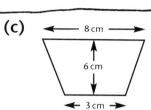
8 cm
6 cm
3 cm
Area = _____

(d)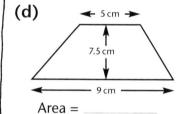
5 cm
7.5 cm
9 cm
Area = _____

(e)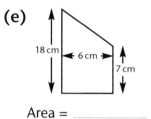
18 cm
6 cm
7 cm
Area = _____

(f)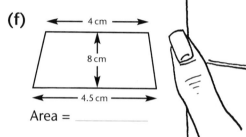
4 cm
8 cm
4.5 cm
Area = _____

(g)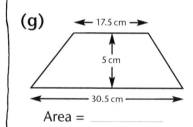
17.5 cm
5 cm
30.5 cm
Area = _____

(h)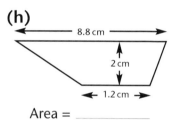
8.8 cm
2 cm
1.2 cm
Area = _____

(i)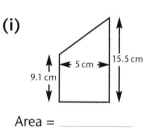
5 cm
15.5 cm
9.1 cm
Area = _____

2. These are the measurements of some cuboids. Use mental methods to find the volume of each cuboid.

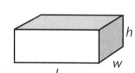

$$\text{Volume of cuboid} = l \times w \times h$$

(a) $l = 9$ cm
$w = 12$ cm
$h = 4$ cm
Volume = _____

(b) $l = 15$ cm
$w = 8$ cm
$h = 6$ cm
Volume = _____

(c) $l = 18$ cm
$w = 3$ cm
$h = 2$ cm
Volume = _____

(d) $l = 12$ cm
$w = 4.5$ cm
$h = 12$ cm
Volume = _____

(e) $l = 17$ cm
$w = 3$ cm
$h = 4$ cm
Volume = _____

(f) $l = 7.5$ cm
$w = 12$ cm
$h = 11$ cm
Volume = _____

NOW TRY THIS!

• Ten right-angled triangular prisms are all different, but each has a volume of 24 cm³.

• Write possible values for l, w and h for the ten prisms.

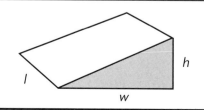

Remember that the volume of any prism is the length multiplied by the area of the end face. Because the area of the end face is a triangle (which is half a rectangle), the volume can be found by using the formula $\tfrac{1}{2} \times l \times w \times h$.

Special measures

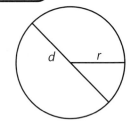

A To find the | circumference | of a circle, multiply the | diameter | by π. This can be written as:

{ Circumference = π × d }   or   { Circumference = π × 2r }

Complete the tables to show the circumference of a circle with each given | radius |. Take π to be **3**.

	Radius of circle	Circumference
(a)	3 cm	18 cm
(b)	2 cm	
(c)	4 cm	
(d)	6 cm	
(e)	10 cm	

	Radius of circle	Circumference
(f)	5 cm	
(g)	7 cm	
(h)	9 cm	
(i)	8 cm	
(j)	12 cm	

B Circular tin lids of different sizes are cut from sheets of metal.

To find the area of a circle, **square** the radius and multiply this by π. This can be written as:

{ Area of circle = π × r × r }   or   { Area of circle = πr² }

Answer these questions mentally. Take π to be **3**.

1. Find the area of each circle in square centimetres.

(a)
3 cm

Area = 27 cm²

(b)
5 cm

Area = _____

(c)
4 cm

Area = _____

(d)
2 cm

Area = _____

(e)
6 cm

Area = _____

(f)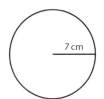
7 cm

Area = _____

(g)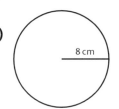
8 cm

Area = _____

(h)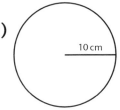
10 cm

Area = _____

2. Find the area of each circle in square millimetres.

(a)
15 mm

Area = _____ mm²

(b)
20 mm

Area = _____

(c)
12 mm

Area = _____

 The **circumference** of a circle is the distance around the edge of the shape. The **diameter** is the width of the circle, from side to side, through the centre. The **radius** is half the diameter (in other words, the distance from the centre of the circle to the edge). Remember: to **square** a number, multiply the number by itself.

Developing Numeracy
Calculations
Year 9
© A & C BLACK

Special measures

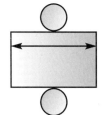

C   A cylindrical aluminium tin is made from two circles and a rectangle, which are welded together.

The **circumference** of each circle is the same length as the rectangle.

1. Answer these questions mentally, with jottings. Take π to be **3**.

For a tin with a **radius** of 3 cm and a height of 10 cm, what is:

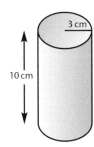

(a) the approximate length of the rectangle? _____

$$Circumference \quad = \pi \times diameter$$
$$= 3 \times \rule{3cm}{0.4pt}$$
$$= \rule{3cm}{0.4pt}$$

(b) the area of this rectangle? _____

(c) the area of each circle? _____

(d) the total amount of aluminium used for this tin? _____

2. Find the total amount of aluminium used to make each of these tins. Take π to be **3**.
Make jottings on paper if you need to.

(a)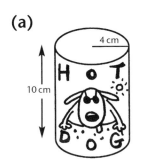

(b)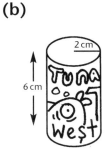

(c)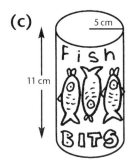

(d)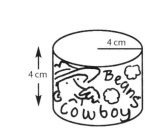

(e)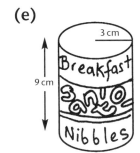

(f)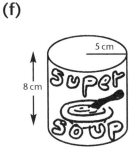

(g)

NOW TRY THIS!

• Find the volume of each of the tins above. Take π to be **3**.

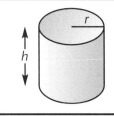

$$\boxed{\text{Volume of a cylinder} = \pi \times r^2 \times h}$$

The **circumference** of a circle is the distance around the edge of the shape. The **diameter** is the width of the circle, from side to side, through the centre. The **radius** is half the diameter. Take care not to confuse surface area with volume. The surface area of these tins is the area of metal used to make them. The volume is the amount of space inside the tin.

Perfect proportions

A

This diagram shows how to convert between percentages, fractions and decimals.

Whatever your starting point, always move clockwise.

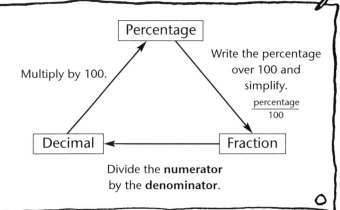

Percentage

Multiply by 100.

Write the percentage over 100 and simplify.

$$\frac{\text{percentage}}{100}$$

Decimal ← Fraction

Divide the **numerator** by the **denominator**.

Complete these conversions. Use the diagram to help you.

(a) 28% is _____ as a fraction

(b) $\frac{2}{5}$ is _____ as a decimal

(c) 0.125 is _____ as a percentage

(d) 0.375 is _____ as a percentage

(e) $\frac{175}{100}$ is _____ as a percentage

(f) 0.005 is _____ as a percentage

(g) 0.48 is _____ as a fraction

(h) 64% is _____ as a fraction

(i) $\frac{6}{5}$ is _____ as a decimal

(j) $1\frac{3}{4}$ is _____ as a percentage

(k) $\frac{171}{100}$ is _____ as a percentage

(l) 0.02 is _____ as a fraction

B

1. Tick to show which adverts are telling the truth. Use mental methods.

New BRILL POWDER
Now over 20% more!
Normally 250 g, now 303 g ☐

New 'Single Decker' bars
1 bar extra – free with this pack of 6!
Over 15% extra free! ☐

LEMON ZEST DRINK
Over 12% more!
1 litre in this bottle
(Normal size 900 ml) ☐

Pay only 12.5% of the RRP!
RRP £8.00 – you pay £1! ☐

Tins now about 21% larger!
Old size 400 ml
Now 484 ml ☐

2. Discuss your answers with a partner.

Remember that the **numerator** is the top number of a fraction and the **denominator** is the bottom number. Give the fractions in their simplest form and as mixed numbers where appropriate. It's a good idea to learn by heart fraction, decimal and percentage equivalents.

Perfect proportions

1. Look at these sketches. The larger one is an enlargement of the smaller one.

Width = 12 cm

Height = 11 cm

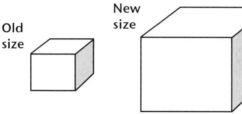

Width = 24 cm

Height = 22 cm

(a) Work out the area of each sketch using mental methods.

Area = _____   Area = _____

(b) How many times larger is the area of the large sketch than the small sketch? _____

(c) What fraction of the area of the large sketch is the area of the small sketch? _____

(d) By what percentage has the area of the small sketch been increased? _____

2. The Acme Novelty Company makes boxes. It decides to enlarge the size of its boxes by changing the dimensions.

Old size

New size

Length = 5 cm
Width = 2.5 cm
Height = 4 cm

Length = 10 cm
Width = 5 cm
Height = 8 cm

(a) By what percentage have the dimensions of the box been increased? _____

(b) Work out the volume of each box, using mental methods.

Old size = _____   New size = _____

(c) How many times larger is the volume of the large box than the small box? _____

(d) By what percentage has the volume of the box been increased? _____

(e) What percentage of the smaller volume is the larger volume? _____

NOW TRY THIS!

| 12% | $\frac{125}{100}$ | $\frac{1}{8}$ | 1.2 | 0.2 | multiplied by | 800 | 80 | 180 |

• Arrange these cards to make 15 different multiplication questions. Use mental methods to find which question has:

(a) the largest answer   **(b)** the smallest answer

Shapes are enlarged by multiplying **each** of their dimensions (for example, length, width and height) by the same number. This number is called the **scale factor**. For both the enlargements above, the scale factor is 2.

Developing Numeracy
Calculations
Year 9
© A & C BLACK

Maths Megabrain!

1. In the Maths Megabrain Quiz, contestants are asked ten mental maths questions. Answer all these questions. Calculate in your head.

Contestant 1

(a) A square has sides of 15 cm.
What is its area? _____

(b) A triangle has a base of 8 cm and a height of 16 cm.
What is its area? _____

(c) A cube has sides of 4 cm.
What is its volume? _____

(d) What is 120 multiplied by 0.01?
_____

(e) What is 8.5 divided by 0.1? _____

(f) What is $5 \times 6 \times 7$? _____

(g) 7200 people went through a turnstile in one hour.
How many per second is this?
_____

(h) If 19×39 is 741, what is 1.9×3.9?
_____

(i) Jack farms 890 acres. One-fifth of this grows corn.
How many acres is this? _____

(j) What is ⁻2.6 multiplied by ⁻50?
_____

Contestant 2

(a) A square has sides of 14 cm.
What is its area? _____

(b) A triangle has a base of 6 cm and a height of 8 cm.
What is its area? _____

(c) A cube has sides of 5 cm.
What is its volume? _____

(d) What is 7.2 multiplied by 200?
_____

(e) What is 0.732 divided by 0.1? _____

(f) What is $5 \times 6 \div 0.1$? _____

(g) 96 cars pass under a bridge each minute.
How many cars per hour is this?
_____

(h) If 2.6×3.5 is 9.1, what is 26×35?
_____

(i) Rachel earns £748 per week and spends one-fifth on travel.
How much is this? _____

(j) What is ⁻3.8 divided by ⁻0.01?
_____

2. The contestants score **2** points for a correct answer and ⁻**1** point for an incorrect answer.

How many questions do they each answer correctly if:

(a) contestant 1 scores 14 points _____   **(b)** contestant 2 scores 5 points _____

Use each of the **factors** of 24, but not 1.
Put each factor into a circle
so that the **products** of the circles
along each line are the same.

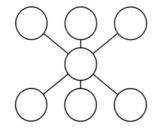

A **factor** is a whole number that divides exactly into another number without a remainder. The factors of 12 are 1, 2, 3, 4, 6 and 12. Remember that you can find the **product** of a set of numbers by multiplying the numbers together.

Developing Numeracy
Calculations
Year 9
© A & C BLACK

C

1.

The rule for this table is A × B + C. Fill in the missing answer.

A	B	C	Answer
4	6	2	26
2	1.5	10	13
6	0.4	1.6	4
5	1.2	10	___

2. Here are some similar tables. You can add, subtract, multiply or divide the numbers in any order. Work out the rule for each table and fill in the missing answers.

(a) Rule = _____

A	B	C	Answer
4	6	2	16
2	1.5	10	17
6	0.4	1.6	6.64
5	1.2	10	___

(b) Rule = _____

A	B	C	Answer
7	35	2	3
8	56	10	−3
9	27	3	0
6	36	4	___

(c) Rule = _____

A	B	C	Answer
5	5	2	20
6	1.5	4	30
1	0.6	2	3.2
5	2	10	___

(d) Rule = _____

A	B	C	Answer
28	6	7	10
9	4	3	7
55	0.4	11	5.4
13	0.75	4	___

(e) Rule = _____

A	B	C	Answer
8	4	8	32
2	7.5	10	5
5	0.4	1.6	6
7	3.5	4	___

(f) Rule = _____

A	B	C	Answer
42	6	6	6
8	1.5	0.5	13
12	4	2	4
35	7	4	___

(g) Rule = _____

A	B	C	Answer
15	5	22	12
2	7.5	10	15.5
5	0.4	1.6	−3
9	1.8	5.2	___

(h) Rule = _____

A	B	C	Answer
8	8	0.5	2
24	1.5	4	4
56	4	2	7
21	3.5	3	___

Winner

NOW TRY THIS!

- Make up three puzzle tables of your own for a partner to solve.

Remember to write down the rules and the missing numbers, but keep them secret.

The rules do not have to use the letters A, B and C in order and they could include brackets: for example, a rule such as (C − B) ÷ A is possible.

Developing Numeracy
Calculations
Year 9
© A & C BLACK

Website statistics

A Here are some statistics about the number of hits on the **poptrivia.com** website.

poptrivia.com

August of this year saw the highest number of hits to date with 10 285.

	Hits	Daily average
May	8176	264
June	9210	307
July	9895	319
August	10 285	332

The most popular time in May for site visits was between 18:00 and 19:00 hours, with approximately 8% of hits.

The most popular time in August this year was between 16:00 and 17:00 hours, with approximately 12% of hits.

The steady rise in the number of hits since August last year (which had a total of 4476 hits) is encouraging.

Use **approximation** and mental methods to estimate these answers.

(a) What is the approximate total number of hits for May, June, July and August together?

_____

Try timing yourself. How long did you take?

(b) Approximately how many more people visited the site in August this year than in August last year?

_____

(c) On a single day in May, about how many people visited the site between 18:00 and 19:00 hours?

_____

(d) On a single day in August this year, about how many people visited the site between 16:00 and 17:00 hours?

_____

(e) If the average daily number of hits for the year (since last August) is about 250, about how many hits did the site receive in the whole year?

_____

poptrivia.com

(f) Using your answer to (e), approximately what percentage of the whole year's hits were made in June?

_____

B Use a calculator to check your estimates to part A.

(a) _____   **(b)** _____

(c) _____   **(d)** _____

(e) _____   **(f)** _____

To use **approximation**, round the numbers in the question to the nearest whole number, ten, hundred or thousand. Being able to make approximations and gain an idea of the approximate size of the answer is a very important skill, particularly when you are working with a calculator. It can help you to realise where you have made a keying-in mistake.

Website statistics

C This pie chart shows the proportion of hits on the **moneyfornothing.com** website during different periods of one day.

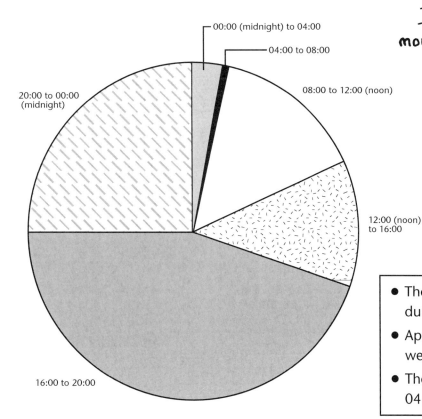

- There were exactly 3947 hits during this day.
- Approximately 12% of the hits were between noon and 16:00.
- There were 34 hits between 04:00 and 08:00.

Use **approximation** and mental methods to estimate these answers.

(a) Approximately what percentage of hits were between 20:00 and midnight? _____

(b) Estimate the number of hits between these times. _____

(c) Approximately what percentage of hits were between 16:00 and 20:00? _____

(d) Estimate the number of hits between these times. _____

(e) Estimate the number of hits between noon and 16:00. _____

(f) Approximately what percentage of hits were between midnight and 04:00? _____

(g) Estimate the number of hits between these times. _____

(h) Circle the answer which most accurately describes the percentage of hits between 04:00 and 08:00.

     15%   less than 1%   9%   86%

(i) Estimate the number of hits between 16:00 and midnight. _____

NOW TRY THIS!

On a different day there were exactly 5000 hits and the pie chart looked the same.

- Estimate the number of hits during each period of time.

 To use **approximation**, round the numbers in the question to the nearest whole number, ten, hundred or thousand. You may find it useful to imagine the circle split into equal slices to help you estimate what fraction (and therefore what percentage of hits) each slice represents.

Estimus Maximus

A

Here is part of a mosaic made with tiles. The tiles are parallelograms, trapeziums, triangles and rectangles. Estimate the approximate area of each tile by rounding the measurements shown. Calculate mentally.

Area of a trapezium = $\frac{1}{2}(a + b) \times h$
a and b are the parallel sides, and h is the perpendicular height. **!**

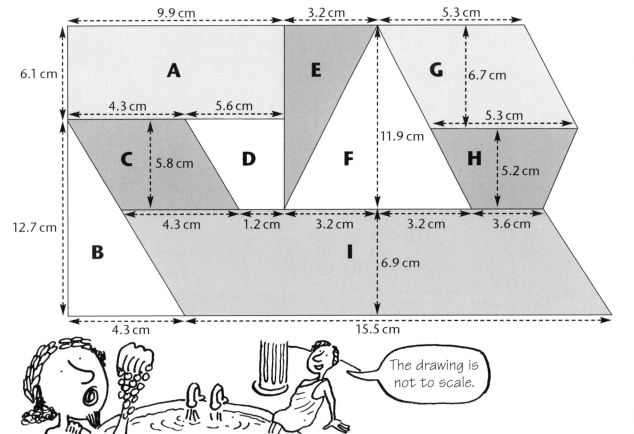

The drawing is not to scale.

Area of A ≈ _10 × 6 = 60 cm²_   Area of B ≈ _____

Area of C ≈ _____   Area of D ≈ _____

Area of E ≈ _____   Area of F ≈ _____

Area of G ≈ _____   Area of H ≈ _____

Area of I ≈ _____   Area of all tiles ≈ _____

Remember: ≈ means 'approximately equals'. **!**

B

1. The decimal points are missing from these answers. Insert them, using **approximation** to estimate the size of the answer. The first is done for you.

(a) 48.6 × 0.18 = 8.7 4 8   **(b)** 84.28 × 6.7 = 5 6 4 6 7 6

(c) 0.71 × 10.7 = 7 5 9 7   **(d)** 425.3 × 125 = 5 3 1 6 2 5

(e) 12 679 ÷ 6.2 = 2 0 4 5 0   **(f)** 256 ÷ 0.16 = 1 6 0 0 0 0

(g) 260.7 ÷ 165 = 1 5 8 0   **(h)** 5640 ÷ 250 = 2 2 5 6

(i) $(15.68)^2$ = 2 4 5 8 6 2 4   **(j)** √(73.6164) = 8 5 8 0

2. Use a calculator to check whether your estimates are sensible.

 To find the area of a **parallelogram**, multiply the base by the perpendicular height. To find the area of a **trapezium**, find the sum of the parallel sides, halve it and multiply this by the perpendicular height. Remember: to use **approximation**, round the numbers in the question to the nearest whole number, ten, hundred or thousand.

Developing Numeracy
Calculations
Year 9
© A & C BLACK

Estimus Maximus

1. Round these numbers and make suitable **approximations**.

(a) $(1094 \div 212) \times 3987$ ≈ *(1000 ÷ 200) x 4000 = 20 000*

(b) $5.75 \times (3.46 - 0.48)$ ≈ _____

(c) $(5895 \div 1967) \times 207$ ≈ _____

(d) $6.34 \times (3.08 + 2.78)$ ≈ _____

(e) $\sqrt{(48.37 - 11.912)}$ ≈ _____

(f) $\sqrt{(8.1 \times 1.98)} + 15.89$ ≈ _____

(g) $(0.03 \times 19.6)^2$ ≈ _____

(h) $(4.5 \div 2.38) \times 9.8$ ≈ _____

(i) $(17.87 \div 2.69) + 17.48$ ≈ _____

(j) $7.88 \times (4.58 \times 4.51)$ ≈ _____

(k) $\dfrac{(5.91 \times 4.09)}{\sqrt{(0.25)}}$ ≈ _____

(l) $\dfrac{(0.41 \times 0.49)}{(0.1)^2}$ ≈ _____

(m) $(0.11 \times 48)^2 \div 4.93$ ≈ _____

Remember:
$0.5^2 = 0.25$

2. Which approximation is better for the question $4.53 \div 2.48$? Tick the box.

Explain your decision. _____

_____

NOW TRY THIS!

- Estimate the **circumference** of a circle with the given **radius**. Take π to be $\frac{22}{7}$.

  (a) Radius = 10.5 cm   Circumference ≈ _____

  (b) Radius = 20.97 cm   Circumference ≈ _____

  (c) Radius = 17.57 cm   Circumference ≈ _____

- 🖩 Use a calculator to check whether your estimates are sensible.

The **circumference** of a circle is the distance around the edge of the shape. The **diameter** is the width of the circle, from side to side, through the centre. The **radius** is half the diameter. Remember: to find the circumference of a circle, multiply the diameter by π. In the 'Now try this!' challenge, check your estimates using the $\boxed{\pi}$ key on your calculator.

A good workout

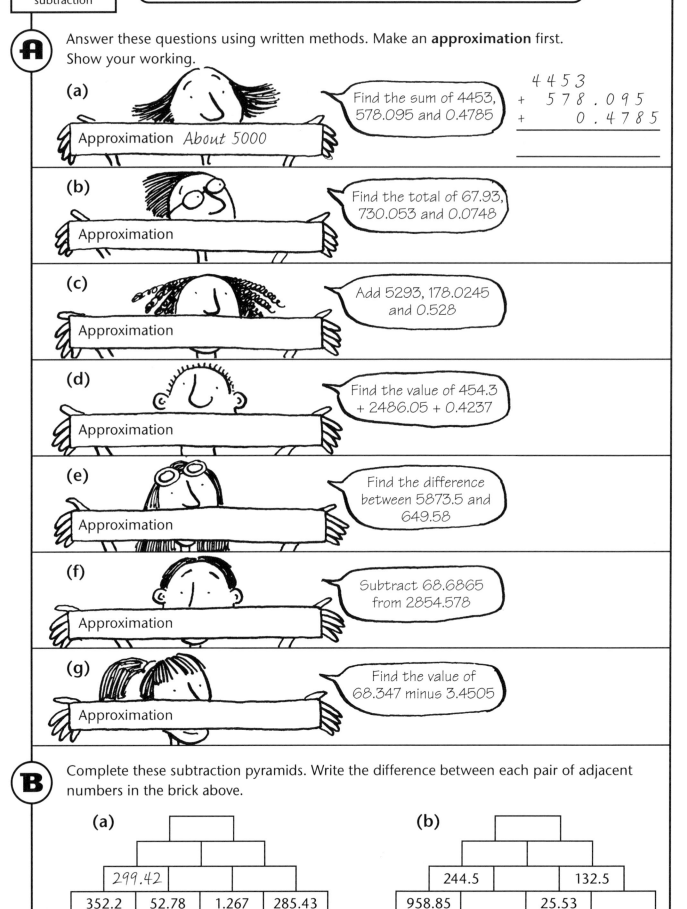

A Answer these questions using written methods. Make an **approximation** first. Show your working.

(a) Find the sum of 4453, 578.095 and 0.4785

Approximation *About 5000*

```
  4453
+ 578.095
+   0.4785
_____
```

(b) Find the total of 67.93, 730.053 and 0.0748

Approximation

(c) Add 5293, 178.0245 and 0.528

Approximation

(d) Find the value of 454.3 + 2486.05 + 0.4237

Approximation

(e) Find the difference between 5873.5 and 649.58

Approximation

(f) Subtract 68.6865 from 2854.578

Approximation

(g) Find the value of 68.347 minus 3.4505

Approximation

B Complete these subtraction pyramids. Write the difference between each pair of adjacent numbers in the brick above.

(a)

	299.42		
352.2	52.78	1.267	285.43

(b)

	244.5		132.5
958.85		25.53	

 To check your answers to the questions on this page, use the inverse operation (for example, use subtraction to check addition, and vice versa). Note that there are different possible solutions to the second subtraction pyramid.

A good workout

C Play this game with a partner. You each need a piece of paper for your workings.

☆ Each choose a question from the bars and cross it off.

☆ Use a written method to answer your question.
If the answer is on the vaulting box, score 1 point.

☆ The winner is the player with the most points when all the questions are crossed off.

349.68 + 49.5 + 0.684	5377 − 26.965
485.104 − 52.516	7897.8 + 478.54 + 0.09
7912 + 294.05 + 0.4965	35.575 + 756.5 + 4.371
789.55 − 57.879	15.29 + 954.2 + 0.785
845.55 + 8785 + 0.256	197.68 + 29.5 + 0.792
8795 − 1382.452	6877.17 − 489.735
2875.8 + 46.2 + 8.594	72.8 + 7915 + 3.244
4628.05 − 458.546	7994.001 − 139.495
4821.001 − 459.58	76.17 − 9.4068
188.57 + 88.5 + 8.2345	98.68 + 49.895 + 3.74
4558.15 − 2845.279	9594.05 − 29.701
7845 + 112.04 + 0.199	1024.08 − 297.831

4169.504	227.972
8376.43	2930.594
731.671	4361.421
5350.035	7854.506
9564.349	8206.5465
152.315	66.7632

My score	My partner's score

NOW TRY THIS! Each letter in the code stands for a digit or a decimal point.

● Substitute digits for the letters. Use a written method to find the answer. Then find what word the digits stand for.

PHONE − MOBILE = _____

.	1	2	3	4	5	6	7	8	9
O	P	L	M	I	R	N	E	B	H

 Remember to make approximations before choosing your questions, as this can help you to select a question with one of the given answers.

Work it out!

A

1. Use a written method to find the area of each rectangle. Approximate first and show your working in the space provided.

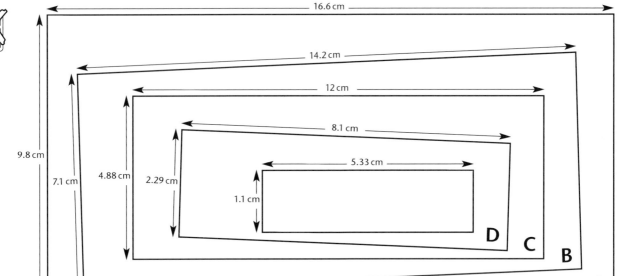

16.6 cm

14.2 cm

12 cm

8.1 cm

5.33 cm

9.8 cm

7.1 cm

4.88 cm

2.29 cm

1.1 cm

D

C

B

A

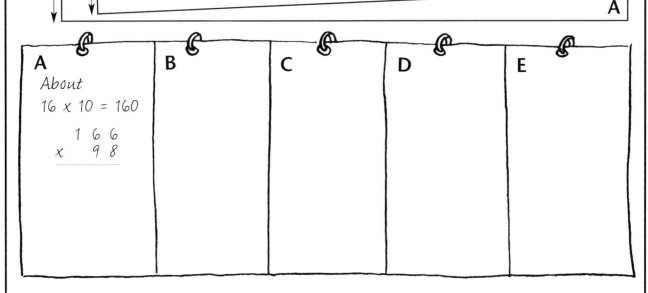

A	B	C	D	E
About 16 × 10 = 160 1 6 6 × 9 8				

Area of **A**:   Area of **B**:   Area of **C**:   Area of **D**:   Area of **E**:

_____ cm²

2. Approximately what fraction of rectangle **C** is rectangle **E**? _____

B

Do these multiplications on paper and tick the correct answer.

(a) 789.8 × 6.5   5133.7 ☐   413.70 ☐   513.37 ☐   4133.7 ☐

(b) 0.262 × 4.6   1.2152 ☐   12.052 ☐   1.2052 ☐   12.152 ☐

(c) 14.6 × 0.049   0.7244 ☐   0.7054 ☐   0.7264 ☐   0.7154 ☐

(d) 34 200 × 0.57   19 494 ☐   1949.34 ☐   20494 ☐   1949.4 ☐

(e) 51 400 × 0.028   1439.2 ☐   1539.2 ☐   143.92 ☐   153.92 ☐

When you are multiplying decimals, it is sometimes easier to make an approximation and then do the multiplication using whole numbers: for example, to answer 8.1 × 5.5 find the answer to 81 × 55. Remember to adjust your answer afterwards by dividing by 10, 100 or 1000 (and so on) as appropriate.

Developing Numeracy
Calculations
Year 9
© A & C BLACK

Work it out!

C These triangles are [similar]. The lengths of the sides of triangle **A** have been multiplied by different **scale factors** to make the corresponding lengths of triangles **B** and **C**.

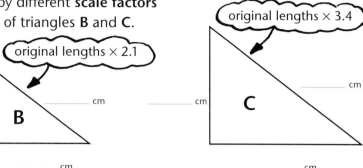

original lengths × 3.4

original lengths × 2.1

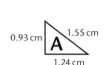
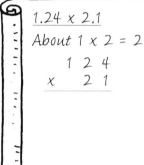

0.93 cm A 1.55 cm
1.24 cm

B ___ cm ___ cm

___ cm C ___ cm

___ cm

___ cm

1. (a) Use written methods to find the lengths of the sides of triangles **B** and **C** (to 2 d.p).

(b) Measure the sides of the triangles to make a rough check of your answers.

Workings

1.24 × 2.1
About 1 × 2 = 2

```
    1 2 4
x     2 1
```

2. An A5 sheet of paper is made by folding an A4 sheet in half.

| A5 | A4 |
| fold |

(a) Use a ruler and find the dimensions of both sheets of paper.

A4: l = _____ w = _____   **A5:** l = _____ w = _____

(b) Use written methods to find whether these statements are true or false.

Each dimension of an A4 sheet is multiplied by just less than 0.71 to get the dimensions of an A5 sheet.   True ☐   False ☐

Each dimension of an A5 sheet is multiplied by just less than 1.42 to get the dimensions of an A4 sheet.   True ☐   False ☐

NOW TRY THIS!

An A4 sheet of paper is made by folding an A3 sheet in half.

• Is the following statement true or false? Test your prediction.

Each dimension of an A4 sheet is multiplied by just less than 1.42 to get the dimensions of an A3 sheet.   True ☐   False ☐

• Now predict what size A0 is. _____

Similar triangles are triangles which have identical angles. The **scale factor** is the number that the dimensions of one triangle are multiplied by to get a similar triangle. For the 'Now try this!' extension, the paper sizes continue in numerical order (A2 is the next size up from A3, then comes A1, and then A0).

Developing Numeracy
Calculations
Year 9
© A & C BLACK

41

Decide – then divide!

A Here are the votes that each contestant on a TV survival show called *Camp Fear* received during one week. The lines were open 24 hours a day, for 7 days.

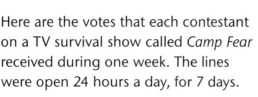

	Phone votes	Text votes
Sam	44 007	58 795
Deepa	125 466	112 356
Claire	54 476	49 478

On a separate piece of paper, use written methods to answer the questions. Give your answers to the nearest whole number.

1. Find the average number of phone votes **per day** for:
   (a) Sam   **(b)** Deepa   **(c)** Claire

   Divide by 7.

6287

2. Use your answers above to find the average number of phone votes **per hour** for:
   (a) Sam   **(b)** Deepa   **(c)** Claire

3. Find the average number of text votes **per day** for:
   (a) Sam   **(b)** Deepa   **(c)** Claire

4. Use your answers above to find the average number of text votes **per hour** for:
   (a) Sam   **(b)** Deepa   **(c)** Claire

B Do these divisions on paper and tick the correct answer.

(a) $389.6 \div 0.8$	587 ☐	487 ☐	497 ☐	507 ☐
(b) $438.9 \div 0.07$	6170 ☐	7170 ☐	6260 ☐	6270 ☐
(c) $0.044 \div 0.0025$	176 ☐	0.266 ☐	17.6 ☐	26.6 ☐
(d) $0.608 \div 6.4$	0.715 ☐	0.095 ☐	0.0715 ☐	9.5 ☐

When you are dividing decimals, it is sometimes easier to make an approximation and then do the division using whole numbers: for example, to answer $32.5 \div 0.6$ find the answer to $325 \div 6$. Remember to adjust your answer afterwards by multiplying or dividing by 10, 100 or 1000 (and so on) as appropriate.

Developing Numeracy
Calculations
Year 9
© A & C BLACK

Decide – then divide!

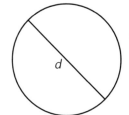

C To find the **circumference** of a circle, multiply the **diameter** by π.
This can be written as:

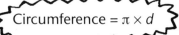

Circumference = π × d

1. Using written methods, complete the tables to show the diameter
of a circle with each given circumference. Take π to be **3.1**.

	Circumference	Diameter
(a)	5.27 cm	
(b)	8.68 cm	
(c)	41.85 cm	
(d)	30.07 cm	

	Circumference	Diameter
(e)	60.76 cm	
(f)	87.11 cm	
(g)	120.28 cm	
(h)	147.87 cm	

2. These two quadrilaterals are **similar**. The sides
of shape **X** have been multiplied by the **scale
factor 7.8** to make the corresponding
sides of shape **Y**.

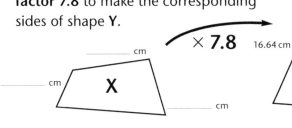

× **7.8**

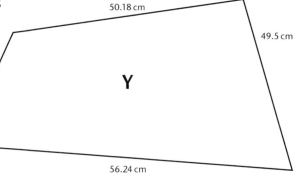

50.18 cm

49.5 cm

16.64 cm

Y

56.24 cm

cm

cm

X

cm

cm

Use written methods to find the lengths of the sides of shape **X**, to 2 d.p.

Workings

NOW TRY THIS!

● Use written methods to find which of these three rectangles has sides closest to 28.5 cm.

(a)

Two sides are each 0.95 cm.
The area is 27 cm².
What is the length of each
of the other two sides?

(b)

Two sides are each 4.9 cm.
The area is 139 cm².
What is the length of each
of the other two sides?

(c)

Two sides are each 0.83 cm.
The area is 24 cm².
What is the length of each
of the other two sides?

The **circumference** of a circle is the distance around the edge of the shape.
The **diameter** is the width of the circle, from side to side, through the
centre. **Similar** quadrilaterals are quadrilaterals which have identical
angles. Remember to make an approximation first to help you be sure that
your answer is about the right size.

Solve it

A

- Maurice Greene broke the indoor 50 m record, running at an average speed of about 9 m per second.
- He held the 60 m record, running at an average speed of about 9.4 m/s.
- He also won a 100 m event, running at an average speed of about 10.2 m/s.

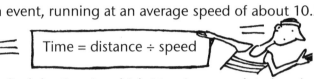

Time = distance ÷ speed

1. Use written methods to find the time in which Maurice completed each race. Give your answers to two decimal places. Show your working.

(a) 50 m	(b) 60 m	(c) 100 m

- A runner takes 8439 seconds to complete a marathon. She travels at a speed of 0.005 km/s.

Distance = speed × time

2. (a) Use this information to find the total length of a marathon in kilometres.

(b) How many **minutes** did this runner take to complete the race?

B

$\boxed{a = 67.3}$ $\boxed{b = 0.07}$ $\boxed{c = 0.045}$ $\boxed{d = 8.3}$ $\boxed{e = 0.0342}$

On a separate piece of paper, use written methods to find the values of the following expressions.

(a) ab = _____

(b) de = _____

(c) ad = _____

(d) bc = _____

(e) cd = _____

(f) $\frac{a}{c}$ = _____

(g) $\frac{a}{b}$ = _____

(h) $\frac{a}{d}$ = _____

(i) $(b + d) ÷ b$ = _____

> Remember:
> $ab = a × b$

!

When **dividing** an integer by a decimal, it is sometimes easier to multiply both numbers by 10 or 100 (for example, 12 ÷ 3.7 has the same answer as 120 ÷ 37). This does **not** work for multiplication, as 12 × 3.7 is not the same as 120 × 37. Instead, treat both numbers as integers (12 × 37) and use approximation to decide where to put the decimal point in the answer.

Solve it

C

1. Use a written method to solve each question. Shade the answers in the grid below.

(a) Bus tickets for a fortnight cost £49.70. What is the cost per day?

(b) T-shirts cost £12.70 each. What is the cost of 27 T-shirts?

(c) Molly cycled for 13 days. She travelled an average distance of 7.85 km per day. What is the total distance cycled?

(d) A year's subscription to a magazine is £93.60. What is the cost per week (given that there are 52 weeks in a year)?

(e) A tin of peas costs £0.38. What is the price of 48 tins?

(f) The total of twenty-five numbers is 78.5. What is the mean?

(g) Rob walked a total of 95.7 km in his 22-day hiking holiday. What is the mean daily distance?

(h) In a 31-day period, Chloe earned £85.25 for babysitting. What is the mean amount earned per day?

(i) Eighteen bottles of hair products cost £67.40. What is the mean cost per bottle (to the nearest penny)?

(j) Twelve suitcases together weigh 235.8 kg. What is the average mass of each case?

£3.55	4.35 km	2601	18.75 kg	£2.57	£2.90
£2.60	£140.48	5.34 km	£8.36	3.14	£1.80
5.6 km	£2.75	£3.74	£342.90	£2.45	6.94
3.75	£18.24	8.3	7.36 km	4.85	6.6
1701	4.85 km	£2.38	102.05 km	4.14	19.65 kg

2. Which is the smallest number left unshaded? _____

NOW TRY THIS!

- Answer these questions and round to one decimal place. Tick the odd one out.

  (a) 75.2 ÷ 24 = _____   **(b)** 0.087 × 36 = _____   **(c)** 78.3 ÷ 25 = _____

- Make up another 'odd one out' puzzle for a partner to solve.

Remember that to find the **mean**, you find the total of the numbers and then divide this by how many numbers there are in the set: for example, the mean of 15, 23, 10 and 16 is (15 + 23 + 10 + 16) ÷ 4 = 64 ÷ 4 = 16.

Shape up!

A

1. Use written methods of division to find the length of each rectangle.

(a)

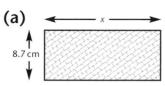

Area = 56.55 cm²   x = _____

(b)

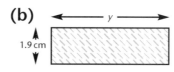

Area = 21.47 cm²   y = _____

(c)

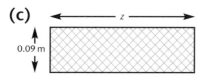

Area = 0.0603 m²   z = _____

(d)

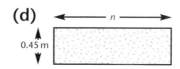

Area = 0.369 m²   n = _____

2. This set of scales measures in both grams and ounces.

(a) Given that the amounts shown on the scales are approximately equivalent, find the number of grams equivalent to 1 ounce.

99.19 g   3.5 oz

1 ounce is 99.19 ÷ 3.5 = _____ g

(b) How many grams are 2.3 oz approximately equal to? _____ g

3. This tape measure shows both centimetres and inches.

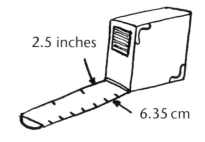

2.5 inches

(a) Given that the amounts shown on the tape measure are approximately equivalent, find the number of centimetres equivalent to 1 inch.

6.35 cm

1 inch is _____ ÷ _____ = _____ cm

(b) How many centimetres are 8.3 inches approximately equal to? _____ cm

B

Use written methods of multiplication to find the volume of each cuboid.

(a)

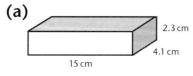

2.3 cm

4.1 cm

15 cm

Volume = _141.45 cm³_

(b)

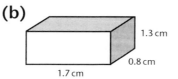

1.3 cm

0.8 cm

1.7 cm

Volume = _____

(c)

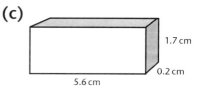

1.7 cm

0.2 cm

5.6 cm

Volume = _____

(d)

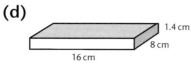

1.4 cm

8 cm

16 cm

Volume = _____

(e)

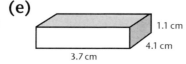

1.1 cm

4.1 cm

3.7 cm

Volume = _____

(f)

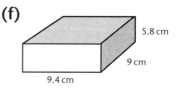

5.8 cm

9 cm

9.4 cm

Volume = _____

Use a separate piece of paper for your written workings. Remember to make approximations before calculating. In part A, questions 2 and 3, round your answers to two decimal places.

Developing Numeracy Calculations Year 9
© A & C BLACK

Shape up!

C

1. Substitute values for *h* and *w* into the formula to find the area.

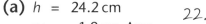

Area of triangle = $\frac{1}{2} \times h \times w$

> Remember, the area of a triangle is half the area of a rectangle.

!

(a) h = 24.2 cm
    w = 1.9 cm Area = ___ *22.9 cm²*

(b) h = 17.8 cm
    w = 4.6 cm Area = ___

(c) h = 32.8 cm
    w = 3.7 cm Area = ___

(d) h = 22.4 cm
    w = 7.8 cm Area = ___

(e) h = 15.7 cm
    w = 8.8 cm Area = ___

(f) h = 19.5 cm
    w = 12.8 cm Area = ___

(g) h = 23.7 cm
    w = 14.6 cm Area = ___

(h) h = 48.2 cm
    w = 16.4 cm Area = ___

h

← *w* →

2. The volume of a triangular prism is the area of the triangular end-face multiplied by the length of the prism. Find the volumes of these prisms.

(a)

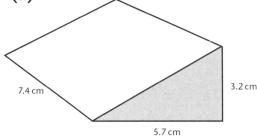

7.4 cm

3.2 cm

5.7 cm

Volume = ___

(b)

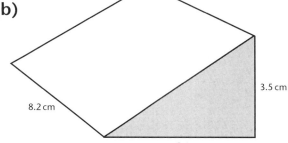

8.2 cm

3.5 cm

5.4 cm

Volume = ___

(c)

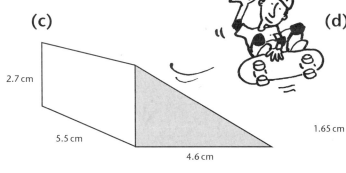

2.7 cm

5.5 cm

4.6 cm

Volume = ___

(d)

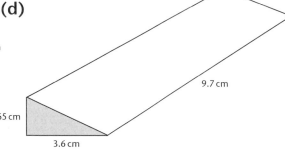

9.7 cm

1.65 cm

3.6 cm

Volume = ___

A three-digit decimal and a two-digit decimal have been made with the digits 2, 3, 4, 5 and 6. One number is divided by the other to get the answer 8.3125.

• What are the two numbers?

 . ÷ ☐ . ☐ = **8.3125**

• 🖩 Check your answers. Explain to a partner how you solved the problem.

 Use written methods for the questions on this page (using a separate piece of paper).

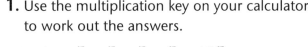

Calculator keys

A

1. Use the multiplication key on your calculator to work out the answers.

(a) $5^4 =$ _5 x 5 x 5 x 5 = 625_   **(b)** $6^4 =$ _6 x_

(c) $2^5 =$ _____   **(d)** $3^5 =$ _____

(e) $4^6 =$ _____   **(f)** $7^6 =$ _____

(g) $8^7 =$ _____

(h) $9^8 =$ _____

(i) $5^9 =$ _____

2. Use the $\boxed{x^y}$ key to answer these questions.

(a) $5^4 =$ _____   **(b)** $6^4 =$ _____   **(c)** $2^5 =$ _____

(d) $3^5 =$ _____   **(e)** $4^6 =$ _____   **(f)** $7^6 =$ _____

(g) $8^7 =$ _____   **(h)** $9^8 =$ _____   **(i)** $5^9 =$ _____

(j) $6^9 =$ _____   **(k)** $3^{10} =$ _____   **(l)** $19^5 =$ _____

(m) $8^7 =$ _____   **(n)** $7^9 =$ _____   **(o)** $13^6 =$ _____

(p) $4^9 =$ _____   **(q)** $16^6 =$ _____   **(r)** $14^5 =$ _____

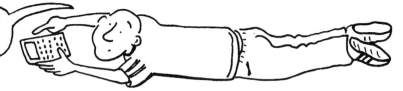

Notice how much quicker and easier it is to use this key!

B

1. Now use the $\boxed{\sqrt[x]{}}$ key to find these roots. Complete the sentences.

(a) $\sqrt[5]{32}$ Which number, when __5__ of them are multiplied together, gives __32__ ?

Answer = __2__ because _2 x 2 x 2 x 2 x 2 = 32_

(b) $\sqrt[4]{1296}$ Which number, when _____ of them are multiplied together, gives _____ ?

Answer = _____ because _____

(c) $\sqrt[5]{243}$ Which number, when _____ of them are multiplied together, gives _____ ?

Answer = _____ because _____

(d) $\sqrt[6]{4096}$ Which number, when _____ of them are multiplied together, gives _____ ?

Answer = _____ because _____

(e) $\sqrt[7]{2187}$ Which number, when _____ of them are multiplied together, gives _____ ?

Answer = _____ because _____

2. Check your answers using the $\boxed{x^y}$ key.

You may have to use the SHIFT key for finding roots. Check your calculator instruction book or ask your teacher if you are not sure how to use these keys on your calculator.

**Developing Numeracy
Calculations
Year 9**
© A & C BLACK

48

Calculator keys

C

1. Find the value of each expression, using the brackets keys on your calculator. Round your answer to two decimal places. Then shade the answer in the grid below.

(a) $\dfrac{46.2 \times 54.2}{12.5 \times (4.7 - 3.6)} =$ _____

(b) $\dfrac{16.8 \times 49.7}{18.4 \times (9.2 - 5.5)} =$ _____

(c) $\dfrac{26.9 \times 38.4}{19.8 \times (7.3 - 2.9)} =$ _____

(d) $\dfrac{22.7 \times 39.7}{15.4 \times (12.4 - 6.9)} =$ _____

(e) $\dfrac{32.7 \times 41.4}{21.6 \times (5.3 - 1.8)} =$ _____

(f) $\dfrac{23.9 \times 37.2}{21.4 \times (10.7 - 3.8)} =$ _____

(g) $2.9 + (8.5 - (12.7 \times 8.4)) =$ _____

(h) $4.5 + (6.9 - (11.7 \times 9.6)) =$ _____

(i) $5.1 + (11.2 - (13.9 \times 12.7)) =$ _____

(j) $7.4 + (8.1 - (9.2 \times 5.4)) =$ _____

(k) $((3.5)^2 + (8.5 - 0.77))^2 =$ _____

(l) $((5.3)^2 + (7.9 - 0.59))^2 =$ _____

(m) $((6.2)^2 + (9.3 - 0.89))^2 =$ _____

(n) $((8.4)^2 + (9.5 - 1.34))^2 =$ _____

(o) $\dfrac{4 \times \sqrt{(3.4^2 + 8^2)}}{5} =$ _____

(p) $\dfrac{6 \times \sqrt{(4.7^2 + 6^2)}}{6} =$ _____

(q) $\dfrac{9 \times \sqrt{(6.9^2 + 7^2)}}{8} =$ _____

(r) $\dfrac{10 \times \sqrt{(8.9^2 + 9^2)}}{9} =$ _____

11.06	13.89	2194.92	7.62	321.85	11.86
273.65	182.11	30.48	12.26	357.26	⁻100.92
229.55	17.91	220.36	1253.16	219.36	10.64
167.90	19.98	32.38	6196.84	⁻2.88	⁻34.18
34.02	⁻160.23	286.67	6.02	20.89	⁻95.28
15.52	14.06	18.89	6.95	10.70	399.20

2. Look at the unshaded sections. What do they spell out? _____

NOW TRY THIS!

$\dfrac{a}{c \times b^2}$

● Tick to show which of these expressions are equivalent to the one above.

$a \div c \div b^2$ ☐ $a \div c \times b^2$ ☐ $a \div (c \times b^2)$ ☐

● Give examples, substituting numbers for a, b and c.

● Make up another puzzle like this for a partner to solve.

 If your calculator does not have brackets keys, you will need to work out the parts in brackets first. When you are using a calculator, it is a good idea to get into the habit of placing it on the table and keying in with your non-writing hand. This will leave your writing hand free to record the answers.

Developing Numeracy
Calculations
Year 9
© A & C BLACK

49

On display

When you are using a calculator, think carefully about the answer on the display.

Do you need to write the answer differently?

Is the question about money?

Is it a time question?

Do you need to round?

A

1. Do these on a calculator and write a sensible answer for each.

(a) £15.78 × 40 = ~~631.2~~   £631.20

(b) £12.36 × 45 = _____

(c) £1230 ÷ 49 = _____

(d) 58p × 22.5 = _____

(e) 87p × 56   = _____

(f) £104 ÷ 272 = _____

(g) £38 ÷ 18   = _____

(h) £57 ÷ 13   = _____

(i) £68 ÷ 18   = _____

(j) £59 ÷ 12   = _____

2. Use the $\boxed{a^{b/c}}$ fraction/decimal key. Enter the number of minutes as a fraction out of 60.

Example: 6 ⌐ 25 ⌐ 60 × 4 = 25.666... or 25 ⌐ 2 ⌐ 3 = **25 hours 40 minutes**

(a) 6 hours 25 minutes × 4 = _25 hours 40 minutes_

(b) 5 hours 25 minutes × 6 = _____

(c) 3 hours 15 minutes × 15 = _____

(d) 5 hours 20 minutes × 10 = _____

(e) 23 hours 6 minutes ÷ 11 = _____

(f) 9 hours 12 minutes ÷ 4 = _____

B

1. Explore these patterns, using the $\boxed{a^{b/c}}$ key.

(a)
$\frac{1}{2} + \frac{1}{4} =$

$\frac{1}{2} + \frac{1}{4} + \frac{1}{8} =$

$\frac{1}{2} + \frac{1}{4} + \frac{1}{8} + \frac{1}{16} =$

$\frac{1}{2} + \frac{1}{4} + \frac{1}{8} + \frac{1}{16} + \frac{1}{32} =$

$\frac{1}{2} + \frac{1}{4} + \frac{1}{8} + \frac{1}{16} + \frac{1}{32} + \frac{1}{64} =$

(b)
$\frac{1}{2} - \frac{1}{4} =$

$\frac{1}{2} - \frac{1}{4} - \frac{1}{8} =$

$\frac{1}{2} - \frac{1}{4} - \frac{1}{8} - \frac{1}{16} =$

$\frac{1}{2} - \frac{1}{4} - \frac{1}{8} - \frac{1}{16} - \frac{1}{32} =$

$\frac{1}{2} - \frac{1}{4} - \frac{1}{8} - \frac{1}{16} - \frac{1}{32} - \frac{1}{64} =$

2. Describe in words what patterns you notice. _____

_____

If the answer to a time question is a decimal, you will need to convert the decimal part of the answer to minutes. To do this, multiply it by 60 (for example, 2.333... hours = 2 hours and 20 minutes).

Developing Numeracy
Calculations
Year 9
© A & C BLACK

On display

1. Convert these times into hours and minutes.

> Multiply the decimal part of the answer by 60 to convert it to minutes.

(a) 954 minutes is the same as _____ hours and _____ minutes.

(b) 744 minutes is the same as _____ hours and _____ minutes.

(c) 1167 minutes is the same as _____ hours and _____ minutes.

(d) 1440 minutes is the same as _____ hours and _____ minutes.

2. Convert these times into days, hours and minutes.

(a) 1546 minutes is the same as _____ days, _____ hours and _____ minutes.

(b) 2892 minutes is the same as _____ days, _____ hours and _____ minutes.

(c) 9121 minutes is the same as _____ days, _____ hours and _____ minutes.

(d) 2881 minutes is the same as _____ days, _____ hours and _____ minutes.

3. Now answer these questions.

(a) Fred's journey to work takes 27 minutes. How long does he spend travelling to and from work in five days? Give your answer in hours and minutes.

(b) Jo's journey to work takes 22 minutes. How long does she spend travelling to and from work in five days? Give your answer in hours and minutes.

(c) Kate's journey to work takes 17 minutes. How long does she spend travelling to and from work in five days? Give your answer in hours and minutes.

(d) Tariq's journey to work takes 16 minutes. How long does he spend travelling to and from work in 20 days? Give your answer in hours and minutes.

(e) Kate's journey to work takes 17 minutes. How long does she spend travelling to and from work on the 241 days a year she works? Give your answer in days, hours and minutes.

(f) Jo's journey to work takes 22 minutes. How long does she spend travelling to and from work on the 238 days a year she works? Give your answer in days, hours and minutes.

4. Check your answers by converting them back to minutes and dividing.

NOW TRY THIS!

• Which card shows the longest time?

| 1 900 800 seconds | 32 400 minutes | 500 hours | 21 days |

• Make up a similar puzzle for a partner to solve.

 To answer questions 2 and 3, remember that you first have to convert the number of minutes to hours and minutes. Then, if necessary, convert the number of hours into days and hours.

Use calculator keys
(π, sign change,
reciprocal)

Press the right key

A

To find the **circumference** of a circle, multiply the **diameter** by π.
This can be written as:

Circumference = π × d   or   Circumference = π × r × 2

> *r* stands for **radius**. **!**

1. Find the circumference (C) of each circle using the $\boxed{\pi}$ key. Round your answers to two decimal places.

(a) 3 cm   **(b)** 5 cm   **(c)** 6.5 cm   **(d)** 7.9 cm

C = _____   C = _____   C = _____   C = _____

To find the area of a circle, square the radius and multiply by π.
This can be written as:

Area of circle = π × r × r   or   Area of circle = πr^2

2. Find the area of each circle using the $\boxed{x^2}$ and $\boxed{\pi}$ keys. Round your answers to two decimal places.

(a) 3.1 cm   **(b)** 5.2 cm   **(c)** 6.4 cm   **(d)** 7.3 cm

Area = _____   Area = _____   Area = _____   Area = _____

B

1. (a) Measure the diameter of each circle in pattern **X**.
   Find the circumferences.

   (b) If the pattern were made out of wire, what would
   be the total length of wire needed? _____

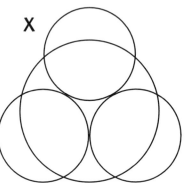

X

Y

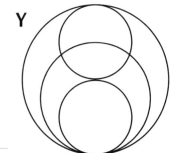

2. (a) Now find the circumference of each circle in pattern **Y**.

   (b) What would be the total length of wire needed? _____

The **circumference** of a circle is the distance around the edge of the shape.
The **diameter** is the width of the circle, from side to side, through the
centre. Notice that you are given the **radius** of each circle in part A.
To find π on your calculator, you may need to use the SHIFT key.

Developing Numeracy
Calculations
Year 9
© A & C BLACK

C Test whether these pairs of expressions are equivalent. Write $=$ or $\neq$ between them, as appropriate.

$\neq$ means that the two expressions are not equal.

(a) $\dfrac{46 \times 24^2}{^-(25^2 + \sqrt{625})}$ ☐ $\dfrac{^-1104 \times (3^3 - 3)}{13 \times 50}$

(b) $\dfrac{\pi \times 8^3}{\pi^2 \times {}^3\sqrt{8}}$ ☐ $\dfrac{64 \times 2^2}{\pi}$

(c) $\dfrac{^-6(4^4 + 1)}{98 + {}^-3}$ ☐ $\dfrac{771 \times {}^8\sqrt{(256)}}{19 \times 5}$

(d) $\dfrac{(^-7)^3 \times (^-2)^5}{\pi \times {}^3\sqrt{27}}$ ☐ $\dfrac{10\,976}{3\pi}$

(e) $\dfrac{\sqrt{(2.5^2 + 5^2)}}{3(^-7 \times \pi)}$ ☐ $\dfrac{\sqrt{(3^3 + 4.25)}}{^-21\pi}$

(f) $\dfrac{^-9 \times {}^3\sqrt{17}}{(^-4)^4}$ ☐ $\dfrac{^-{}^3\sqrt{26}}{^-4^4}$

(g) $\dfrac{2 \times \sqrt{2}}{91 \times 4}$ ☐ $\dfrac{\sqrt{8}}{7(4 + 48)}$

(h) $\dfrac{(1 - 12)(3^4 - 9)}{\pi \times {}^4\sqrt{81}}$ ☐ $\dfrac{88 \times {}^3\sqrt{(^-27)}}{\pi}$

(i) $\dfrac{8(5^2 \times 6^6)}{3\pi}$ ☐ $\dfrac{(^-10)^2 \times 2^7 \times 243}{\pi}$

(j) $\dfrac{8 \times 8^{-1}}{7 \times 7^{-1}}$ ☐ $\dfrac{5973}{3(1990 + 1)}$

(k) $\dfrac{\pi \times 46^2}{(^-6)^4 \times (^-6)^5}$ ☐ $\dfrac{\pi \times 529}{6 \times 4^3 \times 6561}$

(l) $\dfrac{\pi \times \pi^{-1}}{6({}^3\sqrt{4})}$ ☐ $\dfrac{47 \times 49}{48^2}$

(m) $\dfrac{8^4 \times 2^{-1}}{(^-3)^2 \times \sqrt{3}}$ ☐ $\dfrac{(32^2 \times 2)}{\sqrt{243}}$

(n) $\dfrac{5 \times \sqrt{5}}{6 \times \sqrt{6}}$ ☐ $\dfrac{\sqrt{125}}{\sqrt{216}}$

(o) $\dfrac{8^{-1} \times 7^{-1}}{\sqrt{9} \times 4}$ ☐ $\dfrac{(3^{-1} \times 2)}{\sqrt{64} \times 7}$

(p) $\dfrac{8^2 \times \sqrt{8}}{9^2 \times \sqrt{9}}$ ☐ $\dfrac{\sqrt{(4^6 \times 2^3)}}{\sqrt{59\,049}}$

NOW TRY THIS!

- Write an equation to show how to find the **reciprocal** of a number (x). Then use this and the reciprocal key $\boxed{x^{-1}}$ to find the reciprocals of these numbers.

(a) $x = 0.0625$ **(b)** $x = 0.03125$ **(c)** $x = 0.0208333...$

x^{-1} means the same as '1 divided by x' or '$\frac{1}{x}$' and is known as the **reciprocal** of x. When a number and its reciprocal are multiplied together the answer is always 1. Use this to check your answers to the 'Now try this!' challenge.

Developing Numeracy
Calculations
Year 9
© A & C BLACK

53

Private investigations

Programme your calculator to repeatedly add 111, starting with the number 111. Use the [ANS] key or press the [+] key twice.

1. Write the numbers shown on your calculator display in the top rows of these tables. In the row below, write the difference between the last two digits.

111	222	333					
0							
1110							

2. Write about the pattern in the difference between the last two digits of the answers.

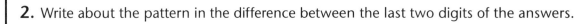

B

1. On a separate piece of paper, add the digits of each multiple of 111. If the answer is a two-digit number, add the digits again. Continue until you reach a single-digit answer. This is called the [digital root].

   Examples: 111 ⟶ 1 + 1 + 1 = 3   444 ⟶ 4 + 4 + 4 = 12 ⟶ 1 + 2 = 3

2. Write what you notice about the digital roots. _____

To perform the constant function with a calculator with an [ANS] key, first input 111 and press [=]. Now press [ANS][+] 111 [=] and keep pressing [=]. On some calculators you can key in 111 [+][+] 111 [=][=][=] for the same effect.

Developing Numeracy
Calculations
Year 9
© A & C BLACK

C

1. (a) Explore these two patterns.

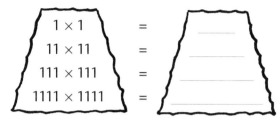

1×1	=
11×11	=
111×111	=
1111×1111	=

9×9	=
99×99	=
999×999	=
9999×9999	=

(b) Predict the answers to these questions.

$11111 \times 11111 =$ _____ $99999 \times 99999 =$ _____

(c) Explain the patterns in words. _____

_____

_____

2. (a) Fill in the multiplication grids for the first pattern above.

11 × 11

×	10	1
10		
1		

111 × 111

×	100	10	1
100			
10			
1			

1111 × 1111

×	1000	100	10	1
1000				
100				
10				
1				

= _121_   = _____   = _____

(b) Discuss with a partner why this pattern occurs.

3. (a) Fill in the multiplication grids for the second pattern above.

99 × 99

×	90	9

999 × 999

×	900	

9999 × 9999

×			

= _____   = _____   = _____

(b) Discuss with a partner why this pattern occurs.

NOW TRY THIS!

- Explore this pattern in the same way. Write a report of things you notice and try to explain why the pattern occurs.

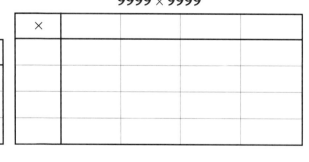

5×5	=
55×55	=
555×555	=
5555×5555	=

For the 'Now try this!' challenge, you may find it useful to draw similar multiplication grids to help you explain the patterns.

Most likely

A

1. For each question, tick the most likely answer and explain your choice.
Approximate first.

(a) 69^2

| 476.1 | 4761 | 47610 |

(b) $42 \div 0.06$

| 700 | 70 | 7000 |

(c) 6.3×5.1

| 2.913 | 29.13 | 32.13 |

(d) $15\,682 - 4897$

| 10785 | 10795 | 9785 |

(e) $8 \div 0.064$

| 0.125 | 125 | 1250 |

(f) 328^2

| 96456 | 92584 | 107584 |

2. Now check your answers **without** using the operation in the question.

B

If you use these cards to make questions starting with the number 1000,
which will give an answer **smaller** than 500? Tick them.

| × 0.1 | × 0.09 | × 1.99 | × 3.4 | × 7.01 | × 0.4 |

| ÷ 6.8 | ÷ 0.6 | ÷ 0.01 | ÷ 0.08 | ÷ 2.7 | ÷ 0.91 |

 In your explanations, you could include references to the units digit, or to other related facts you know.

**Developing Numeracy
Calculations
Year 9**
© A & C BLACK

Most likely

C Play this game with a partner. You each need a copy of this sheet.

☆ Circle the answer you think is correct, **without** working out the exact answer.
You have up to five minutes.

☆ Do this for all the questions, then use a calculator to find the correct answers.

☆ Mark your results.
– If you chose the correct answer, score 10 points!

If you chose a different answer:
– score 2 points if the units digit of your answer is correct
– score 2 points if your answer is within 10 of the correct answer.

For whole number answers:
– score 1 point if your answer is even and the correct answer is even,
 or if your answer is odd and the correct answer is odd.

☆ The winner is the player with the most points.

(a) 452×368	**16 636**	**12 834**	**166 336**	**128 346**	**16 428**
(b) 5.7×4.91	**23.987**	**27 987**	**20.567**	**27.987**	**2.836**
(c) 57^2	**299**	**3259**	**2697**	**83 612**	**3249**
(d) $48 \div 0.06$	**80**	**0.8**	**800**	**672**	**8500**
(e) $\sqrt{1521}$	**49**	**39**	**59**	**19**	**3.9**
(f) $632\,781 + 42\,976$	**1 054 327**	**675 767**	**429 634**	**675 757**	**675 746**
(g) 264^2	**60 696**	**8357**	**49 626**	**65 078**	**69 696**
(h) $1.334 \div 23$	**0.56**	**0.58**	**10.62**	**0.058**	**5.862**
(i) $74 \div 0.032$	**212.5**	**2212**	**2312.5**	**0.212**	**23.5**
(j) $\sqrt{9604}$	**92**	**78**	**88**	**72**	**98**

My score: _____ (out of a maximum of 100)

NOW TRY THIS!

● Join each question to its most likely answer.

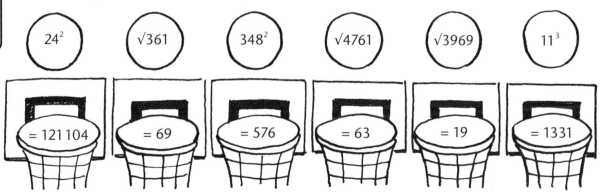

24^2 $\sqrt{361}$ 348^2 $\sqrt{4761}$ $\sqrt{3969}$ 11^3

= 121 104   = 69   = 576   = 63   = 19   = 1331

● Explain how you made your choices.

To work out approximate answers, round the numbers in the question
to the nearest whole number, ten, hundred or thousand, and then do
the calculation using the rounded numbers.

Check it out

1. A shop manager increases the price of a coat by 10%. A few weeks later, she reduces the coat by 10% of its price. Is the coat now the same price as it was before? Tick to show which customer is correct.

Yes.

No, it is cheaper than it was originally.

No, it is more expensive than it was originally.

2. (a) Complete the table. First increase the original price by 10% and write this as the new price. Then decrease the new price by 10% to find the final price.

Original price	Percentage increase	New price	Percentage decrease	Final price
£53	10%	£58.30	10%	
£79	10%		10%	
£131	10%		10%	
£395	10%		10%	
£963	10%		10%	
£15.72	10%		10%	
£26.85	10%		10%	

(b) Compare the original price and the final price. Write what you notice. _____

_____

(c) Explain why you think this is. _____

_____

_____

_____

B (a) On a separate piece of paper, decrease each original price in the table above by 1%.

(b) What do you notice? _____

_____

(c) Explain why you think this is. _____

_____

 In part A, round your answers to the nearest penny.

**Developing Numeracy
Calculations
Year 9**
© A & C BLACK

Check it out

C Mark this homework. Work backwards from the answer each time.

(a) The value of a car decreased by 15% in one year. At the start of the year its value was £5000. What was its value at the end of the year?

£4250 ✔ *£4250 ÷ 5000 x 100 = 85%, which is a 15% decrease so this is correct.*

(b) A car is travelling at 60 miles per hour. If the driver increases the car's speed by 18%, at what speed will the car be travelling?

70.8 mph

(c) The population of a village has decreased by 35% over ten years. Its population ten years ago was 2400 people. What is it now?

1560

(d) A man's mass increased from 54 kg by 12%. What is the man's mass now?

60.48 kg

(e) A businessman earns £16 000 per year. He pays 23% of his salary in tax. How much is left after tax?

£12 320

(f) A businesswoman earns £43 000 per year. She pays 41% of her salary in tax. How much is left after tax?

£25 370

NOW TRY THIS!

- Raz, Ellie and Craig usually get the same amount of pocket money. However, their pocket money goes up or down according to whether or not they do their chores.

(a) Raz: 100% is increased by 40%, then the new amount is decreased by 40%. What percentage of the original amount does Raz receive?

(b) Ellie: 100% is increased by 70% and the new amount is decreased by 70%. What percentage of the original amount does Ellie receive?

(c) Craig: 100% is increased by 99% and the new amount is decreased by 99%. What percentage of the original amount does Craig receive?

- Who receives the most money at the end of the week?

 For question (a) in the 'Now try this!' challenge, first find 40% of 100% and add it on. Then find 40% of this and subtract it to get the final answer.

Answers

p 8

A1 (a) £6.11   (b) £18.97
    (c) £313.74   (d) 118.52
    (e) 292.31   (f) 191.04

A2 (a) Smaller
    (b) Larger

A3 (a) 274.89
    (b) 5742.24
    (c) 2.581
    (d) 16 350
    (e) 2837.5
    (f) 6187.5

B (a) Less than
   (b) Possible answers:

4.8	9.6	14.4
19.2	24	28.8
33.6	38.4	43.2

p 9

C2 (a) Infinitely large   (b) Infinitely small

p 10

B1 (c) Between 0 and 2
    (d) Between 0 and 1
    (e) Between 0 and 1
    (f) Between $^-1$ and 1
    (g) Between 0 and 3
    (h) Between 0 and 1
    (i) Between 0 and 4

p 11

C1 (a) > 14   (b) < 10
    (c) > 15   (d) > $^-15$
    (e) < 4   (f) < 1
    (g) < 1   (h) > 1

C3 (a) < $^-6$ (b) > $^-4$
    (c) > $^-9$ (d) < $^-1$

Now try this!
True statements:

(a) $^-s < ^-1$ $st > s$ $st > t$ $st > 1$ $^-t < ^-1$

(b) $\frac{s}{t} > 1$ $\frac{t}{s} < 1$

p 12

A1 (a) 7.2   (b) 6600   (c) 240
    (d) 360   (e) 2.8   (f) 48
    (g) 660   (h) 81   (i) 56

A2 (a) 180 cm^3 (b) 440 cm^3 (c) 14 cm^3
    (d) 32 cm^3 (e) 13 cm^3 (f) 330 cm^3

B (a) 572
   (b) 442
   (c) 448
   (d) 390
   (e) 990

p 13

C1 (a) $a^2 + 10a + 24$ (b) $b^2 + 9b + 20$
    (c) $c^2 + 12c + 27$ (d) $d^2 + 18d + 77$
    (e) $x^2 + 2xy + y^2$ (f) $y^2 - 1$

C2 (a) $n^2 + 7n + 6$ (b) $n^2 + 9n + 14$
    (c) $n^2 + 9n - 10$ (d) $n^2 - 25$

Now try this!
(a) $n^2 + 4n + 4$
(b) $n^2 + 10n + 25$
(c) $n^2 - 6n + 9$
(d) $n^2 - 22n + 121$

p 14

B1 (a) ✔ (b) ✔   (c) ✗   (d) ✔
    (e) ✗ (f) ✔   (g) ✔   (h) ✗

B2 (a) 2   (b) 4   (c) $\frac{1}{12}$ (d) $\frac{1}{10}$
    (e) $\frac{1}{27}$ (f) 15   (g) 7   (h) $\frac{1}{56}$
    (i) $\frac{1}{121}$ (j) 100   (k) 16   (l) 3

p 15

C1 (a) 0.25   (b) 0.1   (c) 0.125   (d) 0.2
    (e) 0.333   (f) 50   (g) 0.04   (h) 0.056
    (i) 100   (j) 1000   (k) 0.143   (l) 3.333

C3 (a) 16   (b) 0.0625

C4 The number and its reciprocal are inverses, i.e. the reciprocal of a reciprocal is the number itself.

C5 (a) 32   (b) 11
    (c) 43   (d) 28
    (e) 36   (f) 21

Now try this!
64 and 0.015625

p 16

A1 (a) × . 7 =
    (b) ÷ 8 9 =
    (c) × 4 =
    (d) √ =
    (e) x^2 =
    (f) ^{3}√ =
    (g) x^3 =
    (h) ÷ 9 =
    (i) ÷ 7 × 8 =
    (j) × 5 ÷ 9 =

A2 (a) ← + 6 ← × 3 ←
    (b) ← ÷ 7 ← ^{2} ←
    (c) ← – 9 ← ^{3}√ ←
    (d) ← ÷ 4 ← + 0.9 ←

B (a) 16 ÷ 2 + 5 = 13   (b) 6 × 5 – 1 = 29
    (c) 12 + 4 ÷ 8 = 2   (d) 30 – 5 √ = 5
    (e) 3 ÷ $\frac{1}{4}$ × 2 = 24   (f) 13 – 9 squared = 16
    (g) 8 + 2 × 6.4 = 64   (h) 1 – 0.84 √ = 0.4
    (i) 8 × 4 – 5 ^{3}√ = 3

p 17

C1 This activity encourages pupils to appreciate the effect of rounding when using inverses to return to the original number.
    (a) ← cubed ^{3} ← cubed ^{3} ← cubed ^{3} ←
    (b) Yes
    (c) No
    (e) 3, 4, 6, 9 (This may depend on the type of calculator.)

C2 (a) ✔   (b) ✗
    (c) ✔   (d) ✔

Now try this!
(a) $a = 4c + b$ (b) $a = c ÷ b - 5$ (c) $a = \sqrt{c} - b$

p 18

A1 (a) 15   (b) 3
    (c) 9   (d) 1
    (e) 2   (f) 4
    (g) 10   (h) 20
    (i) 2   (j) 5

A2 (a) 12   (b) 28
    (c) 18   (d) 12

B (a) 88.93   (b) 2.60
    (c) 18.96   (d) 125.48
    (e) 42.88   (f) 80.02
    (g) 7.06   (h) 1.78

p 19

C1 False

$(^-3)^2$ means $^-3 \times ^-3 = 9$

$^-3^2$ means $^-(3 \times 3) = ^-9$

C2 Corrected statements:

(a) $(^-a)^2 = 9$

(b) $2a^2 - 7 = 11$

(c) $^-a^2 + 4 = ^-5$

(d) $4a^2 - 1 = 35$

(e) $(^-2a)^2 + 1 = 37$

(f) $3a^2 + 1 = 28$

(g) $^-4a^2 + 4 = ^-32$

(h) $^-5(a^2 - 2) = ^-35$

(i) $(4a)^2 - 5 = 139$

(j) $\sqrt{16} \times a + 1 = 13$

(k) $\sqrt{25} \times a - 11 = 4$

(l) $(\frac{1}{3}a)^3 = 1$

(m) $(7 + ^-2a)^2 = 1$

Now try this!

(a) 55 (b) 47 (c) 227

p 20

A (a) 768

(b) 984

(c) 588

(d) 810

(e) 490

(f) 880

(g) 360

(h) 3366

(i) 588

B (a) 720 (b) 3.6 (c) 0.36

(d) 0.48 (e) 5.6 (f) 64 000

(g) 2800 (h) 0.42 (i) 490

(j) 0.048 (k) 0.27 (l) 0.036

p 21

C1 (a) 30 (b) 40 (c) 36

(d) 100 (e) 56 (f) 44

(g) 20 (h) 3 (i) 16

(j) 20 (k) 7 (l) 3

(m) 72 (n) 90 (o) 112

(p) 1.2 (q) 14 (r) 8

C2 (a) 12 and 4 (b) 14 cm

(c) 13 and 14 (d) 6

(e) $72°$ (f) 350

Now try this!

Example answers:

$\frac{3}{3} \times \frac{3}{3} = 1$

$\frac{3}{3} + \frac{3}{3} = 2$

$3 \times 3 - 3 - 3 = 3$

$(3 \times 3 + 3) \div 3 = 4$

$(3 + 3) \div 3 + 3 = 5$

$3 \times 3 \div 3 + 3 = 6$

$(3 + 3) + \frac{3}{3} = 7$

$3 \times 3 - \frac{3}{3} = 8$

$3 \times 3 \times (\frac{3}{3}) = 9$

$3 \times 3 + (\frac{3}{3}) = 10$

p 22

A1 $\frac{4}{5}, \frac{2}{3}, \frac{7}{9}, \frac{7}{8}, \frac{5}{7}, \frac{8}{9}, \frac{1}{2}, \frac{8}{11}, \frac{23}{25}, \frac{9}{17}, \frac{15}{16}, \frac{1}{37}, \frac{1}{2}, \frac{1}{3},$
$\frac{1}{6}, \frac{18}{25}, \frac{12}{29}, \frac{9}{22}, \frac{13}{19}, \frac{1}{49}, \frac{1}{4}, \frac{5}{5}, \frac{2}{19}, \frac{1}{5}, \frac{1}{6}, \frac{1}{3}, \frac{2}{9}, \frac{4}{9}$

B (a) 28

(b) 12

(c) 14

(d) 12

(e) 18

p 23

C2 54 and 27 (HCF is 27)

Now try this!

HCF = 12

LCM = 72

p 24

A Top number of pyramid:

(a) 8100 (b) 2500 (c) 16 900

B1 (a) £27, £49, £26

(b) £125, £25, £0

(c) £8, £64, £63

(d) £1, £81, £124

(e) £64, £36, £7

(f) £0, £100, £215

B2 (a) Kim

(b) Sam, Kim, Kim

p 25

C1 Top number of pyramid:

(a) 0.04 (b) 0.0004

C2 Top number of pyramid:

(a) 8 (b) 1

C3 (a) 3 (b) 3

(c) 9 (d) 144

(e) 7 (f) 4

(g) 2 (h) 5

(i) 8 (j) 2

(k) 1 (l) 1

Now try this!

64 (or 1)

p 26

A1 (a) 42 cm 108 cm^2

(b) 48 cm 143 cm^2

(c) 46 cm 120 cm^2

(d) 48 cm 128 cm^2

(e) 35 cm 49 cm^2

(f) 35 cm 66 cm^2

(g) 8.6 cm 3.52 cm^2

(h) 26.8 cm 26.4 cm^2

(i) 10 cm 5.25 cm^2

A2 (a) 54 cm^2 (b) 51 cm

(c) 200 cm^2 (d) 24 cm

B1 (a) 192 cm^2

(b) 96 cm^2

(c) 13.2 cm^2

(d) 8.5 cm^2

(e) 45 cm^2

(f) 96 cm^2

B2 5.2 cm

p 27

C1 (a) 30 cm^2 (b) 52 cm^2 (c) 33 cm^2

(d) 52.5 cm^2 (e) 75 cm^2 (f) 34 cm^2

(g) 120 cm^2 (h) 10 cm^2 (i) 61.5 cm^2

C2 (a) 432 cm^3 (b) 720 cm^3 (c) 108 cm^3

(d) 648 cm^3 (e) 204 cm^3 (f) 990 cm^3

p 28

A (a) 18 cm (f) 30 cm

(b) 12 cm (g) 42 cm

(c) 24 cm (h) 54 cm

(d) 36 cm (i) 48 cm

(e) 60 cm (j) 72 cm

B1 (a) 27 cm^2 (b) 75 cm^2 (c) 48 cm^2 (d) 12 cm^2

(e) 108 cm^2 (f) 147 cm^2 (g) 192 cm^2 (h) 300 cm^2

B2 (a) 675 mm^2 (b) 1200 mm^2 (c) 432 mm^2

p 29

C1 (a) 18 cm
(b) 180 cm^2
(c) 27 cm^2
(d) 234 cm^2

C2 (a) 336 cm^2 (b) 96 cm^2 (c) 480 cm^2 (d) 192 cm^2
(e) 216 cm^2 (f) 390 cm^2 (g) 900 cm^2

Now try this!
(a) 480 cm^3 (b) 72 cm^3 (c) 825 cm^3 (d) 192 cm^3
(e) 243 cm^3 (f) 600 cm^3 (g) 1500 cm^3

p 30

A (a) $\frac{7}{25}$ (b) 0.4
(c) 12.5% (d) 37.5%
(e) 175% (f) 0.5%
(g) $\frac{12}{25}$ (h) $\frac{16}{25}$
(i) 1.2 (j) 175%
(k) 171% (l) $\frac{1}{50}$

B1 Lemon Zest advert is incorrect. Other adverts are correct.

p 31

C1 (a) 132 cm^2, 528 cm^2
(b) 4
(c) $\frac{1}{4}$
(d) 300%

C2 (a) 100%
(b) 50 cm^3, 400 cm^3
(c) 8
(d) 700%
(e) 800%

Now try this!
(a) $\frac{125}{100}$ of 800 = 1000
(b) 12% of 80 = 9.6

p 32

A

Contestant 1	Contestant 2
(a) 225 cm^2	(a) 196 cm^2
(b) 64 cm^2	(b) 24 cm^2
(c) 64 cm^3	(c) 125 cm^3
(d) 1.2	(d) 1440
(e) 85	(e) 7.32
(f) 210	(f) 300
(g) 2	(g) 5760
(h) 7.41	(h) 910
(i) 178	(i) £149.60
(j) 130	(j) 380

A2 (a) 8 (b) 5

B Example answer:

p 33

C1 16

C2 (a) $B \times C + A$ 17
(b) $B \div A - C$ 2
(c) $(A + B) \times C$ 70
(d) $A \div C + B$ 4
(e) $(C - B) \times A$ 3.5
(f) $(A - B) \div C$ 7
(g) $B + C - A$ $^-2$
(h) $A \div B \div C$ 2

p 34

A Approximate answers:
(a) 37 000 (b) 6000
(c) 26 (d) 34
(e) 90 000 (f) 10%

B (a) 37 566 (b) 5809
(c) 21.1 (d) 39.8
(e) 91 250 (f) 10.09%

p 35

C Approximate answers:
(a) 25%
(b) 1000
(c) 45%
(d) 1800
(e) 500
(f) 2% − 3%
(g) 100
(h) Less than 1%
(i) 3000

Now try this!
Approximate answers:
00:00–04:00 150, 04:00–08:00 50, 08:00–12:00 700,
12:00–16:00 600, 16:00–20:00 2250, 20:00–24:00 1250.

p 36

A Approximate answers:
A   60 cm^2
B   26 cm^2
C   24 cm^2
D   21 cm^2
E   18 cm^2
F   36 cm^2
G   35 cm^2
H   22.5 cm^2
I   105 cm^2
J   Area of all tiles ≈ 326 cm^2

B1 (a) 8.748 (b) 564.676
(c) 7.597 (d) 53162.5
(e) 2045.0 (f) 1600.00
(g) 1.580 (h) 22.56
(i) 245.8624 (j) 8.580

p 37

C1 Approximate answers:
(a) 20 000
(b) 18
(c) 600
(d) 36
(e) 6
(f) 20
(g) 400
(h) 20
(i) 23
(j) 160
(k) 48
(l) 20
(m) 5

C2 4 ÷ 2
Because the divisor is nearly 2.5, and there are fewer than 2 lots of 2.5 in 4.53. 5 ÷ 2 is greater than 2 so is not the better approximation.

Now try this!
(a) 66 cm^2
(b) 132 cm^2
(c) 110 cm^2

p 38

A (a) 5031.5735
(b) 798.0578
(c) 5471.5525
(d) 2940.7737
(e) 5223.92
(f) 2785.8915
(g) 64.8965

B Top number of pyramid:
(a) 15.243   (a) 112

p 39
Now try this!
PHONE − MOBILE = PROBLEM

p 40
A1 A   162.68 cm^2
B   100.82 cm^2
C   58.56 cm^2
D   18.549 cm^2
E   5.863 cm^2

A2 $\frac{1}{10}$

B (a) 5133.7
(b) 1.2052
(c) 0.7154
(d) 19 494
(e) 1439.2

p 41
C1 (a) Triangle **B**: 1.95 cm, 3.26 cm, 2.60 cm
Triangle **C**: 3.16 cm, 5.27 cm, 4.22 cm

C2 (a) A4: 29.7 cm × 21 cm, A5: 21 cm × 14.8 cm
(b) True, True

Now try this!
True
A0: 120.8 cm x 85.4 cm

p 42
A1 (a) 6287   (b) 17 924   (c) 7782
A2 (a) 262   (b) 747   (c) 324
A3 (a) 8399   (b) 16 051   (c) 7068
A4 (a) 350   (b) 669   (c) 295

B (a) 487
(b) 6270
(c) 17.6
(d) 0.095

p 43
C1 (a) 1.7 cm   (e) 19.6 cm
(b) 2.8 cm   (f) 28.1 cm
(c) 13.5 cm   (g) 38.8 cm
(d) 9.7 cm   (h) 47.7 cm

C2

6.43 cm
2.13 cm   X   6.35 cm
7.21 cm

Now try this!
Rectangle **(a)** is closest (28.42 cm)

p 44
A1 (a) 5.56 seconds
(b) 6.38 seconds
(c) 9.80 seconds

A2 (a) 42.195 km
(b) 140 minutes and 39 seconds

B (a) 4.711   (b) 0.28386   (c) 558.59
(d) 0.00315   (e) 0.3735   (f) 1495.56
(g) 961.43   (h) 8.11   (i) 119.57142

p 45
C1 (a) £3.55   (b) £342.90
(c) 102.05 km (d) £1.80
(e) £18.24   (f) 3.14
(g) 4.35 km   (h) £2.75
(i) £3.74   (j) 19.65 kg

C2 2.38

Now try this!
(a) 3.1333...   (b) 3.132   (c) 3.132
Question **(a)** is the odd one out.

p 46
A1 (a) 6.5 cm   (b) 11.3 cm
(c) 0.67 cm   (d) 0.82 cm

A2 (a) 28.34 g
(b) 65.18 g

A3 (a) 2.54 cm
(b) 21.08 cm

B (a) 141.45 cm^3 (b) 1.768 cm^3 (c) 1.904 cm^3
(d) 179.2 cm^3 (e) 16.687 cm^3 (f) 490.68 cm^3

p 47
C1 (a) 22.99 cm^2 (b) 40.94 cm^2
(c) 60.68 cm^2 (d) 87.36 cm^2
(e) 69.08 cm^2 (f) 124.8 cm^2
(g) 173.01 cm^2 (h) 395.24 cm^2

C2 (a) 67.488 cm^3 (b) 77.49 cm^3
(c) 34.155 cm^3 (d) 28.809 cm^3

Now try this!
53.2 ÷ 6.4

p 48
A1 (a) 625   (b) 1296
(c) 32   (d) 243
(e) 4096   (f) 117 649
(g) 2 097 152
(h) 43 046 721
(i) 1 953 125

A2 (a) 625   (b) 1296   (c) 32
(d) 243   (e) 4096   (f) 117 649
(g) 2 097 152 (h) 43 046 721 (i) 1 953 125
(j) 10 077 696 (k) 59 049   (l) 2 476 099
(m) 2 097 152 (n) 40 353 607 (o) 4 826 809
(p) 262 144   (q) 16 777 216 (r) 537 824

B1 (a) 2
(b) 6
(c) 3
(d) 4
(e) 3

p 49
C1 (a) 182.11   (b) 12.26
(c) 11.86   (d) 10.64
(e) 17.91   (f) 6.02
(g) ⁻95.28   (h) ⁻100.92
(i) ⁻160.23   (j) ⁻34.18
(k) 399.20   (l) 1253.16
(m) 2194.92   (n) 6196.84
(o) 6.95   (p) 7.62
(q) 11.06   (r) 14.06

C2 A1

Now try this!
$a \div c \div b^2$
$a \div (c \times b^2)$

p 50
A1 (a) £631.20   (b) £556.20
(c) £25.10   (d) £13.05
(e) £48.72   (f) £0.38
(g) £2.11   (h) £4.38
(i) £3.78   (j) £4.92

A2 (a) 25 hours 40 mins
(b) 32 hours 30 mins
(c) 48 hours 45 mins
(d) 53 hours 20 mins
(e) 2 hours 6 mins
(f) 2 hours 18 mins

B1 (a) $\frac{3}{4}$ $\frac{7}{8}$ $\frac{15}{16}$ $\frac{31}{32}$ $\frac{63}{64}$
(b) $\frac{1}{4}$ $\frac{1}{8}$ $\frac{1}{16}$ $\frac{1}{32}$ $\frac{1}{64}$

B2 In (a), denominators are multiplied by 2; numerators are always one less than the denominator. In (b), denominators are multiplied by 2; numerators are always 1.

p 51

C1 (a) 15 hours 54 mins
    (b) 12 hours 24 mins
    (c) 19 hours 27 mins
    (d) 24 hours

C2 (a) 1 day, 1 hour and 46 minutes
    (b) 2 days and 12 minutes
    (c) 6 days, 8 hours and 1 minute
    (d) 2 days and 1 minute

C3 (a) 4 hours 30 mins
    (b) 3 hours and 40 mins
    (c) 2 hours and 50 mins
    (d) 10 hours and 40 mins
    (e) 5 days, 16 hours and 34 mins
    (f) 7 days, 6 hours and 32 mins

Now try this!
32 400 minutes

p 52

A1 (a) 18.85 cm   (b) 31.42 cm
    (c) 40.84 cm   (d) 49.64 cm

A2 (a) 30.19 cm   (b) 84.95 cm
    (c) 128.68 cm   (d) 167.42 cm

B1 (a) 11.94 cm, 7.85 cm, 7.85 cm, 7.85 cm
    (b) 35.5 cm

B2 (a) 6.28 cm, 9.42 cm, 12.56 cm
    (b) 28.26 cm

p 53

C (a) =   (i) =
  (b) =   (j) =
  (c) ≠   (k) ≠
  (d) =   (l) ≠
  (e) ≠   (m) =
  (f) =   (n) =
  (g) =   (o) ≠
  (h) =   (p) =

Now try this!
(a) $\frac{1}{x} = 16$ (b) $\frac{1}{x} = 32$ (c) $\frac{1}{x} = 48$

p 54

A1 Pattern of differences of last two digits, where × means 'lots of':
9 × 0
9 × 1
1 × 9
8 × 2
2 × 8
7 × 3
3 × 7
6 × 4
4 × 6
10 × 5
4 × 6
6 × 4
3 × 7
7 × 3
2 × 8
8 × 2
1 × 9

B1 3, 6, 9, 3, 6, 9...

B2 They are all multiples of 3.

p 55

C1 (a) 1, 121, 12321, 124321
    81, 9801, 998001, 99980001
    (b) 123454321, 9999800001

C2 (a) 121, 12321, 1234321

C3 (a) 9801, 998001, 99980001

p 56

A1 (a) 4761
    (b) 700
    (c) 32.13
    (d) 10 785
    (e) 125
    (f) 107 584

B × 0.1, × 0.09, × 0.4, ÷ 6.8, ÷ 2.7

p 57

C (a) 166 366
  (b) 27.987
  (c) 3249
  (d) 800
  (e) 39
  (f) 675 757
  (g) 69 696
  (h) 0.058
  (i) 2312.5
  (j) 98

Now try this!
$24^2 = 576$
$\sqrt{361} = 19$
$348^2 = 121\,104$
$\sqrt{4761} = 69$
$\sqrt{3969} = 63$
$11^3 = 1331$

p 58

A1 No, it is cheaper than it was originally.

A2 (a) Final prices:
    £52.47
    £78.21
    £129.69
    £391.05
    £953.37
    £15.56
    £26.58

    (b) The final price is less than the original price.
    (c) 10% of the new price is greater than 10% of the original price.

B 10% of 100% is 10%. This is added.
   10% of 110% is 11%. This is subtracted.
   So the final answer is 1% less.

p 59

C2 (a) – (f) All answers are correct.

Now try this!
(a) 84%   (b) 51%   (c) 1.99%
Raz